Don't Be Stupid. Pay Attention, Damn It!

Other Books by James P. Rowles

Law and Agrarian Reform in Costa Rica[1]

El onflicto Honduras-El Salvador- de1969 y el orden jurídico international (The Honduras-El Salvador Conflict of 1969 and the International Legal Order)[2]

Don't Be Stupid.
Pay Attention,
Damn It!

Advice for Undecided Voters and Voters Leaning Toward Trump

James P. Rowles

Trenchant Observer Press
San Francisco
2024

Trenchant Observer Press
San Francisco

Mailing Address
P.O. Box 3271
Half Moon Bay, CA 94019

IngramSpark editions
979-8-9901590-8-2 (paperback)
979-8-9901590-9-9 (ePub)

Book design by Michael Grossman
Cover painting by Octavious Sage
Author Photo by Gerard Lum

Dedication

To

Molly Faraji, my companion

Russell R. Rowles, my father
Mildred Shotwell Rowles, my mother

Zaida Arguedas, my former wife

Gordon A. Craig,
John Henry Merryman, and
Abram Chayes,
my mentors

Edward M. Kovachy, Jr., my coach

And to the millions of people, including readers of this
book, who long for and believe in a future governed by
domestic and international law, and by reason and truth

Admonition

And yet, we are oppressed by one nightmarish idea: ***if a dictatorship in Hitler's style should ever rise in America, all hope would be lost for ages.*** [emphasis added] We in Germany could be freed from the outside. Once a dictatorship has been established, no liberation from within is possible. Should the Anglo-Saxon world be dictatorially conquered from within, as we were, there would no longer be an outside, nor a liberation. The freedom fought for and won by Western man over hundreds, thousands of years would be a thing of the past. The primitivity of despotism would reign again, but with all means of technology...

–Karl Jaspers, *The Question of German Guilt*[3]

Table of Contents

Preface

After the publication of *The Rape of American Democracy: Republican Actions and Democratic Failures, 2016-2021* on September 18, 2024, I woke up one Saturday morning (on September 14. 2024) with one burning idea in my head: Publish *Don't Be Stupid, Pay Attention, Damn It! Advice for Undecided Voters and Voters Leaning Toward Trump.*

The idea for the book came from a column I had just published in *Trenchant Observations*, my Substack newsletter (jamesrowles.substack. com). Less than six weeks after the idea occurred to me on that Saturday morning, this book is being published. That is both a tribute to my extraordinary book designer, Michael Grossman, and to my extraordinary artist, Octavius Sage, who began work on the cover painting while he was on vacation in Michigan. It is also a tribute to the extreme urgency the author felt with the November 5, 2024 presidential and congressional elections only weeks away. While this book will be of continuing relevance after the November elections, it is obviously of immediate relevance to those elections.

As of mid-October 2024, the polls suggested that the presidential race was a toss-up.

How could that be? This book addresses that question, and many others related to it.

How, in America in 2024, could we be facing a situation remarkably similar to that faced by citizens in Germany between November 1932 and February 1933?

A friend, in a pessimistic mood, remarked to me. "As America appears to be like a powerless steamboat which is being carried by the current and will go over an enormous waterfall on November 5, I can at least tell my children and grandchildren that while I was not in Germany in November 1932-Frebruary 1933, I was in the United States from October 2024 through January 2025.

The title of the book says a great deal about the current political situation in America, as does the painting on the cover.

As these words are being written, in October 2024, America approaches what is perhaps the most decisive day in the country's history since the Civil War.

The political situation is highly fraught with uncertainty.

On the one hand, it is painful to realize that perhaps half the electorate in America today leans toward voting for a fascist leader who, in the words of General Mark Milley, the former Chairman of the joint Chiefs of Staff of the U.S. military, he is "a fascist to the bone",

Bob Woodward, in his new book *War*, (New York: Simon & Schuster, 2024, published on October 15, 2024), reports on a conversation he had with Geneal Milley at a reception in Washington on March 6, 2023, as follows:

"We gotta talk," General Milley said as I approached him.

...

"No one has ever been as dangerous to this country as Donald Trump, Milley said, "Do you realize, do you see what this man is?"

...

"We have to stop him!' Milley said "You have got to stop him'By you' he. meant the press broadly. "He is the most dangerous person ever. I had suspicions when I talked to you about his mental decline and so forth, but now I realize he is a total fascist. He is the most dangerous person in this country,"

...

"A fascist to the core!!" Milley repeated to me.

I will never forget the intensity of his worry.

The chapters in this book, as was the case in *The Rape of American Democracy*, are based on information that was publicly available at the time they were written. The author drew on highly reliable sources, which may be directly accessed by clicking on a link in the Kindle or ePub (eBook) edition of the book.

Instead of the usual approach in which events are reported from the point of view of the present moment, when the outcomes of events are known, these chapters present events and questions which key actors faced with all of the uncertainties of the moment when such future outcomes were unknown. This gives the reader a sense of the drama of unfolding events and the high stakes and hopes and fears associated with them. The result is more like a motion picture than a completed painting.

This book should be of continuing interest and relevance long after the elections on November 5, 2024. For it contains lessons that might be learned, both to understand what has happened and is happening in America, and to guide citizens' actions in the future.

In a country where up to half of the electorate is prepared to vote for a fascist Leader, regardless of the outcome of the November elections, Americans will have to deal for a long time to come with the fascist threat represented by Donald Trump and his supporters, including the Republicans in what has become a fascist party under the total control of its Leader, Donald Trump.

Introduction

Public Discourse in America

To understand how half or more of the electorate, particularly in battleground states, could be committed or leaning toward voting for Donald Trump on November 5, 2024, it is useful to consider certain changes in American society that have taken place over the last 50 or 75 years.

These changes, moreover, have taken place against the broader background of even deeper changes that occurred in Europe and the United States in the previous century, as described by José Ortega y Gasset in his prescient work. *The Revolt of the Masses.* (1930)[4] "The rebellion of the masses," he wrote, should not be understood as having "a meaning excessively or primarily political. "Public life," he wrote,

> is not solely political, but equally, and even primarily, intellectual, moral, economic, religious; it comprises all our collective habits, including our fashions both of dress and of amusement.

It is against this background that we must understand the following changes in American society over the last 50 or 75 years.

First, participation in civic organizations and civic life has plummeted during this period.

See Robert D., Putnam, *Bowling Alone: The Collapse and Revival of American Community,* rev. ed., 2000.[5]

Second, the public's ability to listen to and be guided by expert opinion has decreased sharply.

> *See* Tom Nichols, *The Death of Expertise: The Campaign Against Established Knowledge and Why It Matters,* 2nd ed., 2023.[6]

To be sure, anti-intellectualism and distrust of experts is not new in American political life.

> *See* Richard Hofstadter, *Anti-Intellectualism in American Life,* 1966.[7]

Third, civic education and knowledge of government, politics, and the world has greatly diminished.

> *See* Richard Haass, *An Introduction to the World,* 2023, pp. xv-xx.[8]

Fourth, the addiction to social media and the Internet among the young, and others, has had a detrimental impact on the ability of citizens to participate in reasoned debate.

> *See* Franklin Foer, *World Without Mind: The Existential Threat of Big Tech,* 2017.[9]

During the period covered by *The Rape of American Democracy: Republican Actions and Democratic Failures, 2016-2021* and by this book (2022-2024), the era in which Donald Trump dominated media coverage—in the 2016 presidential race, during the Trump Presidency (2017-2021), in its immediate aftermath (2020-2021), and in the subsequent years liading up to the November 2024 presidential election, it seemed that many Americans came to question the very concept of truth, as Donald Trump and his supporters dismissed any news article critical of Trump and his supporters as simply "fake news."

However, as Timothy Snyder has pointed out, democracy depends on truth.

See Timothy Snyder, *On Tyranny: Twenty Lessons from the Twentieth Century*, 2017.[10]

Snyder expresses the fundamental relationship between truth and freedom in stark terms, as follows,

Believe in Truth

To abandon facts is to abandon freedom. If anything is true, then no one can criticize power, because there is no basis on which to do so. If nothing is true, then all is spectacle. The biggest wallet pays for the most blinding lights.[11]

He observes further,[12]

As observers of totalitarianism such as Victor Klemperer[13] noticed, truth dies in four modes, all of which we have just witnessed.

The first mode is the open hostility to verifiable reality, which takes the form of presenting inventions and lies as if they were facts...

The second mode is shamanistic repetition...As Klemperer noted, the fascist style depends upon "endless repetition," designed to make the fictional plausible and the criminal desirable...

The next mode is magical thinking, or the open embrace of contradiction.... Accepting untruth of this radical kind requires a blatant abandonment of reason....

The final mode is misplaced faith…. Once truth had become oracular rather than factual (in Nazi Germany), evidence was irrelevant…

In the broader arc of history, we can see the impact of the shift from a culture of public discourse based on the written word to one based on entertainment and the values of television and the TV commercial. Neil Postman, in his classic book, *Amusing Ourselves to Death* (1985), describes this fundamental shift from an age of the printed word, which began with the invention of the printing press by Johannes Gutenberg around 1450, and what Postman calls the Age of Entertainment, which began with television in the 1950s and which now continues both on television and on the Internet.

See Neil Postman, *Amusing Ourselves to Death: Public Discourse in the Age of Show Business*, 1985, 20th ed. 2006.[14]

In a world of political discourse dominated by the values of entertainment and television, one can begin to understand the impact of the social changes which have led to the present situation. These social changes have made phenomena like Donald Trump possible and opened the door to his election in 2016 and the threat of his potential reelection in 2024.

The implications for politics are grave. Writing in 1985, as if seeing through a crystal ball, Postman warns:

When a population becomes distracted by trivia, when cultural life is redefined as a perpetual round of entertainments, when serious public conversation becomes a form of baby-talk, when, in short, a people become an audience and their public business a vaudeville act, then a nation finds itself at risk: culture-death is a clear possibility.[15]

Now, in August 2024, the United States faces one of the most fateful decisions in its history. Will the voters elect former President Donald Trump, a felon convicted of 34 counts of fraud by a Manhattan jury and who is awaiting trial on numerous other felony counts?[16] Will they elect a compulsive liar, someone found guilty of sexual assault by a jury in a civil proceeding in New York, and a political leader who has consistently demonstrated his sympathies for Vladimir Putin and Russia? Will citizens vote for Trump and for the Republican candidates for the House and the Senate, almost all of whom have prostrated themselves before Trump, who has remade the Republican Party in his image?

Or will they vote for the Democrats, and a return to a normal government, and legislators who are focused on solving the many problems which Americans face today?

Given the irrational factors that can affect mass opinion and how voters decide to cast their ballots, one cannot be sanguine about the outcome of the elections in November. In considering how to vote, voters would be well advised to consider the events between 2016 and 2021 described in this book.

The selection of Kamala Harris to be the Democratic candidate for president in 2024, and her subsequent choice of Minnesota Governor Tim Walz to be her running mate have given hope to Democrats who only weeks earlier were nearly despondent over the likely victory of Donald Trump as president and Republican candidates in the House and the Senate in November.

The challenge which Harris and Walz face remains formidable, however.

In any world where voters were guided by reason, Harris and Walz would trounce Donald Trump, J.D. Vance, and their MAGA supporters. Unfortunately, we don't live in such a world. The challenge Kamala Harris must now face is how to reach and persuade those Trump supporters and potential supporters who are not guided by reason, but rather by mass political emotions. Harris and Tim Walz, her vice-presidential candidate, must also build up a sufficient lead so that the election will not be thrown to Trump and the Republicans by some huge, unexpected event, as discussed further below.

This Book

The key slogan among members of Bill Clinton's campaign in 1992 was, "It's the Economy, Stupid". This slogan helped mobilize campaigners and direct them to maintain their focus on economic issues, which were those of greatest concern to voters in 1992. The slogan was coined by campaign adviser James Carville. Clinton's focus on the economy is credited with helping him win the election that year.

The Democrats need James Carville now. In the changed electoral world of 2024, the decisive issue in the 2024 presidential election might be summed up by Carville today in the slogan, "It's Immigration, Stupid".

Trump is hammering Harris on this issue, appealing in the crudest manner possible to the emotions of susceptible voters and their subconscious fears of immigrants taking over America.

Harris, prisoner perhaps of immigrant factions within the Democratic Party and her supporters, has not acted effectively to deal with these subconscious fears. The demographics of the country *are* changing, but Harris has failed to come up with any dramatic program of action to deal with those fears.

Trump has used the issue to great effect.

Unfortunately, there is little evidence to suggest that officials in the Kamala Harris campaign understand this fundamental point. Nor do they seem to understand how effectively Donald Trump is using Nazi propaganda techniques to drive home the issue, and to persuade voters that he is the only candidate who can protect them from the invading hordes of illegal criminal immigrants.

That is the reason why Trump and vice-presidential candidate J.D. Vance have doubled down on their monstrous lie that illegal Haitian immigrants are stealing pet dogs and cats in Springfield, Ohio, *and eating them*. It is the reason why Donald Trump campaigns in Aurora, Colorado maligning those he labels "illegal criminal immigrants" who he falsely asserts are taking over towns like Aurora, Colorado across the country.

These are the same techniques Adolf Hitler used in whipping up hatred of the Jews.

Trump and his propagandists are successfully employing propaganda techniques identified by Adolf Hitler in *Mein Kampf,* and brilliantly used by Hitler and his propaganda minister, Joseph Goebbels, during his ascent to power in January 1933 and throughout the Third Reich (1933-1945).

Donald Trump's rise to power has been similar in many ways to that of Hitler, particularly through the use of propaganda and The Big Lie, which in Trump's case was that he won the 2020 presidential election which had been stolen from him through massive fraud.

The chapters in this book address numerous aspects of Donald Trump's rise to power as president (2017-2021), as Leader of a growing authoritarian movement, and as the Republican candidate for the presidency in 2024. Trump is using all methods—*any* methods—to regain power and the White House, whether by winning the election fair and square, or by trying to seize power through a coup d'etat as he tried to do with his unsuccessful conspiracy and attempt to overthrow the election in 2020-2021.

One important difference from his coup attempt on January 6, 2021 is that he is not Commander-in-Chief and does not have control over the military. That control will remain in the hands of President Joe Biden until January 20, 2025. Any risk of a coup would not arise, therefore, until after Trump is inaugurated should he be elected.

Trump is a desperate man. If loses the election on November 5, 2024, he may spend the rest of his life in prison.

How did America come to this point?

Continuing the narrative in *The Rape of American Democracy: Republican Actions and Democratic Failures, 2016-2021*, the chapters in this book bring the story up to date, on the eve of the November 5, 2024 presidential and congressional elections.

Whatever the outcome of those elections, the chapters in this book will provide important historical context and lessons learned about the rise of the fascist movement led by Donald Trump, for years to come.

Lessons learned from the events described in this book will be of continuing interest to scholars, officials, journalists, and citizens long after the November elections. Importantly, the developments described here should also be of continuing interest to students of American politics, in classrooms in colleges and universities across the United States, and indeed in other countries where the battle to resist fascism is imminent or already joined.

Part One

Don't Be Stupid.
Pay Attention, Damn It!

September 10, 2024

Advice for Undecided voters or Those Leaning Toward Trump

Don't be Stupid! Pay Attention, Damn It!

Advice for undecided voters: Pay attention, damn it! If you are undecided at this stage of the election cycle, you have not been paying attention.

The first duty of every citizen in a democracy is to inform themselves, to the best of their ability, about the candidates and the issues in the election.

If you have been lazy and are leaning toward or committed to voting for Trump and the Republicans because you are simply following the mass emotions of your tribe, there is still time for you to inform yourself and be a patriot. You can still be a good citizen who takes his duties and responsibilities seriously.

And if you have children, you can still be a parent who makes them proud, and of whom they will be proud in 20 years. You can still be a model for them of a good citizen, one who takes his responsibilities as a citizen in a democracy seriously.

What is the point of a debate with a proven liar?

What is the point of such a debate before many "low information" and credulous voters who have no memory, and therefore no basis to determine whether what the candidate says is true or false?

What can we learn from the presidential debate tonight?

1. That there is no more important qualification to be president of the United States than honesty.

And

2. That in the most fundamental sense, the presidential race is about character.

Key questions you should ask

1. Ask yourself: Who would you choose to run your business, head your church, or run your school? Who would you choose to babysit or otherwise care for your children?

2. Why would you vote for a candidate of such known and proven dishonesty, dishonesty that would disqualify the candidate from almost any job?

3. Why would you vote for a convicted criminal who has also been indicted by independent grand juries for the commission of many serious felonies, in the District of Columbia, Georgia, and Miami, Florida?

4. If you believe these indictments are the product of a "witch hunt" and without merit, have you read the charges?

See, e.g., Melissa Murray and Andrew Weissmann, *The Trump Indictments: The Historic Charging Documents with Commentary* (New York: W.W. Norton & Company, 2024).

5. Have you seriously tried to find out if such a "witch hunt" in fact exists, and whether the charges against the candidate are groundless, as he maintains?

Investigate the facts.

Wake up and pay attention!

Part Two

Donald Trump and the Fascist Threat

2

May 14, 2020

Why Trump Is Likely to Win in November (2020)

As things are going now, President Donald J. Trump is likely to be reelected in the November 2020 presidential election.

It is important to understand why this is the case, if Democrats and others are to have any chance of increasing their prospects for victory in the election of the person who will be president until January 20, 2025.

Why is Trump likely to be reelected?

First, he is a political genius.

This is a fact that Democrats do not understand, and do not want to accept. Only a political genius could have achieved the support in the polls which Trump has maintained, given his record of crimes, abuses of power, and other malfeasance in office.

His malfeasance in office includes, most notably, his mishandling of the coronavirus epidemic, leading to the greatest economic catastrophe since the Great Depression and a death toll which now exceeds 80,000 people, and is likely to exceed 150,000-200,000 Americans by November 2020.

Trump has spent his entire life observing and trying to manipulate the media. He polished his sense of how the crowd responds emotionally to events during his 15 years (2004-2017) running *The Apprentice* on NBC. He has learned how to dominate each daily news cycle and continues to do so very effectively. With this power, he is able to distract public attention from reporting on his malevolent policies and misdeeds, and endlessly create new controversies that keep him in the spotlight while avoiding serious and sustained consideration of his lies and lawlessness.

Politically, he has sensed the deep emotional desire in the population to escape from the COVID-19 lockdown, physical-distancing, and mask restrictions. After much hesitation, inaction and dismissal of the seriousness of the pandemic, Trump reluctantly appeared to accept the advice of epidemiological experts and other scientists to urge lockdowns and other social restrictions—belatedly, and always with a wink and a nod to those who opposed such measures. In the end, however, he has finally and ultimately come down on the side of "opening up" the country, ignoring the warnings of his experts.

This appears to be politically astute. He will be able to campaign on the platform that he is and has always been the advocate of the working man (or woman) who wants to get back to work. In doing so, he will be appealing to a massive and deep emotional longing on the part of most people in the United States.

The fact that 200,000 people may die as a result of such an approach does not appear to be a matter of concern, either to the president or to the great masses of Americans from which he draws his supporters.

Second, Trump is likely to be reelected because of his successful use of mass political propaganda. He has led a largely successful war on the concept of Truth, at least among Republicans and other supporters.

Third, Trump has been conducting a successful and sophisticated social media operation, which operates effectively in spreading his propaganda. In comparison, Democrats and Biden are dead-in-the-water. There is a lack of decisiveness in Biden's campaign, which has not even been able to resolve its conflict with Michael Bloomberg's Snapfish company over who should be in charge of the campaign's social medial operations.

Fourth, Trump has been leading a successful process of *Gleichschaltung* (synchronization of views and positions) in taking total control of the Republican Party.

Fifth, he is the incumbent, and exercises all of the powers of the presidency.

Other factors pointing to a likely Trump victory include a lack of funding for the Democrats' social media operations, and the failure of the House Democrats to take on Trump directly through a broad impeachment inquiry.

Democrats appear clueless regarding the fact that Trump is beating them with his appeals to and manipulation of mass emotions. They don't understand how Trump's furtherance of a world of irrationality advances his objectives, whereas their own appeals to reason seem to have already reached the reachable and are now dismissed by broad masses of people who are tired of experts and reason.

3

February 12, 2021

The Cancer on the American Body Politic

Let there be no doubt about it. The American body politic is infected by a cancer. That cancer threatens the existence and survival of American democracy. Currently all of the antibodies and forces defending the body politic are fully engaged in fighting the cancer.

The cancer on the American body politic must be killed, with the political equivalents of chemotherapy, radiation, and even surgery where necessary.

Unlike a human body, the American body politic does not have the expected lifespan of a single human being. In the case of an individual fighting cancer, remission for five or ten years might, in some cases, be regarded as a "success." This is not the case with the American body politic, however. A five-or-ten-year remission of the cancer would not be sufficient to save the life of a democracy that is already 244 years old.

The cancer on the American body politic is represented by the current Republican Party, and most but not all of its senators and representatives in Congress.

The cancer is represented by the overwhelming majority of Republican voters, throughout the country, who have been seduced by a false god who demands idolatrous obeisance to his absolute will.

It is represented by the universe of lies and delusions to which Republican voters have subscribed, and by the determination of these same cult followers to impose their will, the leader's will, on their elected senators and congressmen.

The Trial of 50 Republican Senators

The guilt of ex-president Donald J. Trump for the high crimes and misdemeanors for which he is being tried in the Senate, following his impeachment by the House of Representatives, has been clearly established by the House impeachment managers. His defense team has not resorted to serious legal argument. We know that there can be no defense for the actions he has taken, in full sight, and which have been shown to us in video and slides and other evidence in the last three days.

We know that the Republican Party is already guilty of having supported Trump's attempted coup and remained silent or endorsed his Big Lie that he won the November 3 election.

Two of these 50 Republican senators reportedly helped lead the insurrection on January 6, which included not only the mob action in invading the Capitol but also the legislative rebellion of Republican congressmen and senators who, without the slightest legal justification, tried to block the certification of the Electoral College vote which named Joe Biden President.

Josh Hawley will forever be remembered for his raised fist in the air as the insurrectionist mob headed toward the Capitol. Sitting in the gallery of the Senate during the trial of Donald Trump, ostentatiously ignoring the proceedings, a man of high intelligence and low moral character, he must know that his political career is over. Ted Cruz, another of the ringleaders, has already begun to take on the appearance of a grizzled old man who, at the moment of truth, chose to step on the wrong side of history and to betray his country.

Moments of Truth

There have been some incredible moments of truth during and since the Capitol Insurrection. U.S. Capitol Police Officer Eugene Goodman, confronting a mob of insurrectionists in the Senate corridors, chose to act with courage in the face of great potential harm and single-handedly led the mob away from the Senate Chamber. He also ran to head off Senator Mitt Romney from walking into the mob and into great danger as he was moving forward.

Goodman had but a split second to make his choice. Almost instinctively, he chose to act with courage and honor, with heroism really. Hawley and Cruz had more time to make their choice, between honor and country, on the one hand, and cowardice, treason and betrayal of country, on the other. They made the wrong choice.

Now, 50 Republican senators face a similar moment of truth. Will they honor their oaths of office to uphold the Constitution and to defend their country against all enemies foreign and domestic "so help me God"? Will they honor their solemn oaths to do impartial justice in accordance with the Constitution and laws in the impeachment trial of Donald J. Trump, "so help me God"?

Or will they betray their oaths, the American people, and their country, kowtowing and genuflecting instead before the false god who threatened our democracy, who attempted to stay in power through a coup d'état, the last act of which was the Capitol Insurrection?

As a columnist, you wish you had the power to craft words that would sway Republican senators to honor their oaths of office and their oaths to serve as impartial jurors in the impeachment trial. But you know that they have sold their souls to the Devil, that they have entered into Mephistophelean bargains they hope will give them continued political life, just as Goethe's Faust sought to prolong his earthly life.

You know they have sold their souls to the false god Trump and his "base" of idolaters. You know also that they live in fear, fear of the Trump mob, fear of the fascist leader and his fascist followers. You know also that this is no excuse.

Once honorable men and women perhaps, most of them have now followed Trump's path as co-conspirators, as men and women who, observing monstrous lies and great evil, looked away and said nothing.

Their place in the history books is almost secure. Their individual names will long be forgotten, like the names of the corrupt Tammany Hall gang that once ruled New York. But their actions will live forever in infamy.

One Last Shot at Redemption

These 50 Republican senators have one last shot at redemption: they can honestly evaluate the charges in the article of impeachment and weigh the evidence, which will lead them ineluctably to a decision to convict Donald Trump for his attempted coup and the Capitol Insurrection on January 6, 2021.

With a vote for conviction, they will also be voting to excise the source of the cancer from the American body politic.

Will they do it? The odds are long against such an epiphany at this late hour. But who knows?

The final decision is one which each person can make only in the innermost recesses of their own heart and soul. As did Officer Eugene Goodman, they face a moment of truth, a fateful decision involving polit-ical danger if not the danger of life or death. They can choose between courage and their country, honoring their oaths, on the one hand, and cowardice and treason, on the other.

Their decisions will mark their lives and careers for all time. It is as if their children and grandchildren, and further descendants could read on their tombstones, "He (or she) voted to honor his (or her) oaths and to save the Republic," or "He (or she) voted to betray the Constitution and his (or her) country, and for the false god Donald Trump." Which will be their epitaph?

Throughout their lives, they will have to face their children and grand-children, and everyone they know or may come to know, and answer that question.

If they make the wrong choice, the shame of that choice will mark them for the rest of their days.

FURTHER READING

1) "In Memoriam: The Republican Party (March 20, 1854-February 13, 2021)," *The Trenchant Observer*, February 16, 2021;[17]

2) "Fascism in America Is Here NOW, in the Republican Party," *The Trenchant Observer*, May 20, 2021;[18]

3) Michael Gerson, "The Threat of Violence Now Infuses GOP Politics. We Should All Be Afraid," *Washington Post*, May 20, 2021 (2:48 p.m. EDT).[19]

4

May 2, 2021

When Will Trump Be Indicted?

When will Trump be indicted?

We have an apparent serial felon on the loose, hanging out at or near Mar-a-Lago in Palm Beach, Florida.

He is the unnamed "Individual One" in the indictment of Michael Cohen, who is currently serving out a sentence after pleading guilty, on August 21, 2018, to campaign finance violations, tax fraud, and bank fraud. Numerous reports from reliable sources point to Trump as "Individual One," who the Cohen indictment said had ordered Cohen to commit the crimes. It should have been a simple matter to unseal the identity of "Individual One" in the Cohen indictment, and to simply fill in Donald Trump's name and indict him. Why hasn't that happened?

Robert Mueller in his report lists at least ten cases where Trump appears to have committed obstruction of justice. The evidence Mueller cites sounds convincing. Why have indictments not been issued in these ten cases?

Donald Trump was impeached in 2019 for obstruction of justice, which included a number of crimes. During and after the House impeachment investigation, Trump appears to have committed further crimes involving obstruction of justice, including witness tampering and retaliation against witnesses for truthfully testifying in the House investigation. Why has Trump not been indicted for these crimes?

In December 2020, Trump was impeached a second time for his actions related to inciting an insurrection that included, but was not limited to, the invasion of the Capitol by a mob, which resulted in the deaths of at least five people. Why has Trump not been indicted for the crimes that lay at the heart of his impeachment for the Capitol Insurrection?

The political decision by Republican senators not to remove him from office constituted a violation by them of their oaths of office and their oaths to render "impartial justice" as jurors in the impeachment trial. But their decisions, which were politically motivated, in no way absolved Trump of criminal responsibility for the crimes he apparently had committed.

From the summer of 2020 until November 3, 2020, Trump engaged in a number of actions that would appear to have been serious crimes

After the election, on November 3, 2020, Donald Trump appears to have engaged in multiple crimes, ranging from attempts to corrupt election officials responsible for counting and tallying the votes, and attempts to persuade legislators and governors to violate election laws and constitutional provisions for the election of the president. These actions culminated in the Capitol Insurrection on January 6, 2021, and the president's own apparent incitement to insurrection on that day. His failure to send National Guard troops to protect the lives of Vice President Mike Pence, House Leader Nancy Pelosi, and other legislators and their staffs—withholding such assistance for some three hours—evidenced not only his callous indifference but probably also his intent to promote the insurrection.

Putting all of these actions together, it appears that Donald Trump led a vast conspiracy in which he enlisted the support and cooperation of Republican federal, state, and local legislators and officials, to overthrow the results of the November 3 presidential election and, consequently, the Constitution of the United States.

Why have we heard virtually nothing about federal or state grand juries investigating these alleged crimes?

There have been only a few exceptions, such as the grand jury in Atlanta where a courageous prosecutor is investigating a blatant case of apparent election interference for which there is recorded and public evidence.

Why indeed has former President Donald Trump not yet been indicted for the many crimes he has apparently committed? When will he be indicted?

Moreover, when will his many Republican co-conspirators and accomplices in these apparent crimes be investigated and themselves indicted?

What is going on?

We are all tired of thinking about Trump and his crimes. However, democracy is a very fragile flower, and we have just seen how close we can come to losing it, to seeing it crushed. If America's first fascist president, and the many members of the Republican Party who engaged in a vast conspiracy to overthrow the Constitution, are not held accountable before the courts for the very numerous crimes which they appear to have committed, the lesson of political impunity will not be lost on others, while these unpunished actors, apparent criminal co-conspirators, will remain in power to commit further crimes in the future, whether in 2022 or 2024.

Americans who are too cowardly to defend American democracy by prosecuting, and insisting on the prosecution of, those who have committed criminal acts in furtherance of the Republican conspiracy to overthrow the Constitution, will have only themselves and their own passivity to blame if that democracy is lost.

FURTHER READING

1) "The U.S. Doesn't Need Investigations or Commissions. It Needs Prosecutions, *The Trenchant Observer*, May 28, 2021;[20]

2) Laurence H. Tribe, "Trump's Crime Spree Must Not Escape Investigation; The Presidency Must Never Become a Get-Out-of-Jail Free

Card for All Crimes Committed in One's Lifetime," *Boston Globe*, Updated January 4, 2021 (4:30 p.m.);[21] See also Laurence H. Tribe, Barbara McQuade, and Joyce White Vance, "Here's a roadmap for the Justice Department to follow in investigating Trump," Washington Post, August 5, 2021 (9:10 a.m. EDT);[22]

3) Ankush Khardori, "What the DOJ Isn't Telling Us about Jan. 6; Merrick Garland Can and Should Be More Forthcoming about Investigating the Insurrection," *Politico*, July 6, 2021 (12:00 p.m. EDT).[23]

4) "Trump's Future," *The Trenchant Observer*, January 18, 2021.[24] This article cites Anne Applebaum's interview in *Die Welt* on January 18, 2021, in which she declares, "Trump's adventure is over. He will spend the rest of his life in court."

5) Laurence H. Tribe, Barbara McQuade, and Joyce White Vance, "Here's a roadmap for the Justice Department to follow in investigating Trump," Washington Post, August 5, 2021 (9:10 a.m. EDT);[25]

6) Laurence H. Tribe, "Merrick Garland must investigate Donald Trump's attempted coup — not for retribution but for deterrence; For nearly all of us, a solid factual basis that one has committed a federal crime — much less inciting an insurrection against the government itself — would trigger a criminal investigation. So why the hesitation by the US attorney general?" Boston Globe, Updated August 20, 2021 (2:49 p.m.);[26]

5

June 2, 2021

Sleepwalking in the Garden of Fascism: "Merrily We Roll Along!"

Merrily We Roll Along
by Eddie Cantor

Merrily we dance along while facing the sun
Merrily our slogan is: 'say, don't we have fun?'
We live in style, with a smile and a song
As we merrily roll along!

Reading the newspapers and watching cable news, one would think that life is moving along, merrily moving along, and that all is well in the United States.

President Joe Biden is pushing his initiatives, while he appears to have that old-fashioned belief that good deeds and policies will be rewarded by voters at the polls.

The House Democrats are continuing merrily along their path, now planning some kind of further investigation into the Capitol Insurrection on January 6.

At the Justice Department, prosecutors are moving merrily along with their endless investigations into what are essentially peripheral matters.

Attorney General Merrick Garland, who at his confirmation hearings swore that he would not allow political considerations to influence the work of the Justice Department, and in particular decisions whether or not to prosecute individuals, seems to be moving merrily along.

Newspapers have relegated threats to American democracy to the periphery of their attention, while op-eds seem to focus on secondary subjects, the kind of subjects that would merit attention if everything in America were moving merrily along.

This is the way the guardians of democracy, in the press, in the Congress, and in the White House, appear to be moving merrily along.

What could possibly go wrong?

Republicans are working hard, in seeming unison, to pass voter suppression laws and electoral laws that would give state officials and legislators the power to overthrow the results of popular elections, as some Republican officials tried to do in 2020.

Democratic and non-Trump-compliant Republican officials appear to be influenced by threats of physical harm to themselves and their families. The threat of political violence in the country seems to lie just below the surface, while mass shootings appear to have become almost a daily occurrence.

What could be wrong?

What could possibly go wrong?

Former President Donald Trump and numerous co-conspirators and presumptive felons run around freely, with no fear of arrest or prosecution.

Everyone seems quite undisturbed by the non-prosecution of politicians in high places who have committed serious and blatant crimes, in broad daylight.

Trump introduced the normalization of the unthinkable, and the normalization of the unforgivable.

The Biden administration and Attorney General Garland are now introducing the normalization of impunity for politically motivated crimes at the highest levels.

House Democrats should forget the immense distraction of conducting yet another investigation of the insurrection on January 6.

Instead, they should be holding hearings into why the Biden administration and the Justice Department are not prosecuting serious felonies committed by the former president and his Republican co-conspirators, who sought to overthrow the election and the Constitution of the United States.

The country faces a stark choice between prosecuting the presumptive criminals, who committed their crimes in broad daylight, or accepting the normalization of impunity for political crimes at high levels, as the country rolls merrily along.

If America chooses the second path, what could possibly go wrong?

6

June 21, 2021

The Normalization of Impunity: The Story No One Will Cover

When will Trump be indicted?

Why are we asking this question five months after Democratic President Joe Biden has been in office?

A Pulitzer Prize is waiting for the newspaper or magazine that will field a news team to take this story on.

The Biden administration and Merrick Garland's Justice Department have not convened grand juries and indicted Donald Trump and his Republican co-conspirators for the many electoral crimes and other crimes they committed in what amounted to a vast Republican conspiracy to overthrow the election and the Constitution.

All the attention has been diverted to the insurrection on January 6 and the violent demonstrators who seized the Capitol. Attention of the media has focused on the foot soldiers and not the generals who sent them into battle. Trump and his Republican co-conspirators committed many acts of intimidation of election officials and other acts of obstruction of justice. Why have Biden and Garland not prosecuted these crimes?

Many of these questions can be summarized in a single question: Why has Trump not been indicted?

Yet there is perhaps an even more important question in a fading democracy with a weakened press whose priorities are set, at least on cable TV stations, by how much soap the TV programs can sell.

Why isn't the press reporting on the failure of Biden and Garland to investigate and prosecute Donald Trump and his co-conspirators?

See, "America Has Become a Country of the Absurd," *The Trenchant Observer*," June 6, 2021.[27]

There, we observed,

"It is as if some foreign country that is an enemy of democracy had launched a massive missile attack on the United States that unleashed a tasteless, odorless gas on the entire population, causing total amnesia regarding certain tenets of democracy and the rule of law.

"One such bedrock principle of the rule of law is that crimes must be punished, suspected criminals must be indicted and tried, and, when found guilty, sent to prison.

"In the absurd country which America has become, however, the feckless Democrats have become complicit in *the NORMAL-IZATION OF IMPUNITY* for high public officials who commit political crimes while in office.

"If Trump gave us *the Normalization of the Unthinkable* and *the Normalization of the Unforgivable*, President Joe Biden and Attorney General Merrick Garland have given us *the Normaliza-tion of Impunity.*"

Which newspaper or magazine or news team will go after the Pulitzer that is just sitting there, like on a table, waiting for someone to pick it up?

7

July 6, 2021

Denazification and Detrumpification

Updated November 2, 2021

The United States faces a problem similar in many ways and different in many ways to the problem faced by Great Britain, France, and the United States after the defeat of Adolf Hitler and the Nazis in May 1945.

Denazification

In their respective occupation zones—which included parts of Berlin—England, France, and America faced the daunting task of governing a population whose thinking and world view had been altered by 12 years of Nazi lies and propaganda and the terror with which the Nazi regime had ruled as it seized all positions of power and influence in the country.

The cult of Adolf Hitler was very strong. The Western Allies needed to de-program the German population in their respective occupation zones as a first step toward laying the groundwork for a future democratic state and society.

The Western Allies held certain advantages, including military occupation and control over all governmental decisions in the British, French, and American zones of occupation and their respective sectors in Berlin.

Importantly, they also held control over all means of mass communication, including newspapers and radio.

With these advantages, they launched a program of what was known as denazification, portrayed brilliantly in the movie "Judgment at Nuremberg." In addition to the trials of the major war criminals in Nuremberg, they held denazification trials of Nazi leaders and other officials in 12 different sectors of government. Leon Jaworski, the prominent Houston lawyer who later became the famous Watergate Prosecutor, was an American prosecutor in one or more of the lower-level trials of Nazi war criminals.

The Saturday Night Massacre

On Saturday, October 20, 1973, President Richard Nixon ordered Attorney General Elliot Richardson to fire Special Prosecutor Archibald Cox. Richardson refused and resigned effective immediately, as did Deputy Attorney General William Ruckelshaus when he was ordered to fire Cox. These events produced a firestorm of reaction. The impeachment proceedings against Nixon began ten days later, on October 30, 1972, and Leon Jaworski was sworn in as the new Watergate Special Prosecutor on November 1, 1973.

Detrumpification

The situation in the United States in July 2021 is vastly different from the situation the Western Allies faced in Germany in 1945.

Nonetheless, there is a strong need to carry out a program of detrumpification.

While Donald Trump and the Republicans were defeated at the polls on November 3, 2020, Trump refused to admit his defeat, launching the

Big Lie that he won by a landslide and that the election was "stolen" by Biden and the Democrats through massive fraud.

The official results showed that Trump was defeated in the Electoral College by a vote of 306-232 electors. The popular vote results were 81,283,098 votes for Joe Biden, or 51.3 percent of the votes cast. Trump won 74,222,958 votes, or 46.8 percent of the votes cast.

See James M. Lindsay (The Water's Edge blog), "The 2020 Election by the Numbers," *Council on Foreign Relations*, December 15, 2020 (5:00 p.m. EST).[28]

Every electoral process aimed at verifying the results of the elections, including decisions by some 60 courts, have completely rejected all arguments of fraud on any scale that might have remotely affected the outcome of the elections. Interestingly, the Republicans do not challenge the elections that gave them 50 Senate seats and a pickup of a number of seats in the House of Representatives.

On January 6, 2021, even after the Capitol Insurrection, eight Republican senators voted against certification of the electoral votes of Arizona and/or Pennsylvania, while 128 Republicans in the House of Representatives opposed certification of the electoral votes of one or more states, notwithstanding the certification by the Electoral College vote on December 14, 2020. Before the Capitol Insurrection, some 14 senators and 140 Republican members of the House were reportedly planning to vote against certification.

See,

1) Jenny Gross and Luke Broadwater, "Here Are the Republicans Who Objected to Certifying the Election Results," *New York Times*, January 7, 2021 (Updated January 8, 2021);[29]

2) Li Zhou, "147 Republican Lawmakers Still Objected to the Election Results after the Capitol Attack; Congress Has Certified President-Elect Joe Biden as the Winner of the Election — but Some Republicans Still Objected," *Vox* (vox.com), Updated January 7, 2021 (3:28 p.m. EST).[30]

Li Zhou reports, "In a vote Wednesday evening, six Republicans in the Senate and 121 in the House backed objections to certifying Arizona's electoral outcome, while seven Senate Republicans and 138 House Republicans supported an objection to certifying Pennsylvania's electoral outcome."

Gradually, all but a very small minority of Republican senators and congressmen came to endorse the Big Lie and to adopt it as a litmus test for good standing in the Republican party. The Republican caucus expelled Wyoming Representative Liz Cheney from her position as the third-ranking member of the House Republican leadership because she refused to endorse the Big Lie. She was replaced by Elise Stefanik (R-New York), a shameless Trump sycophant who did.

Republicans at the state level have also endorsed the Big Lie and plan to "primary" those who haven't done so in the upcoming 2022 elections.

The corruption of the Republican party has been almost complete, including at the state level and among Republican candidates for election to state-wide political office.

Far from controlling the news media as the Western Allies did in Germany after World War II, the victorious Democrats face a mass media machine headed by Fox News, which propagates the Big Lie and spreads many other lies to tens of millions of Trump and Republican supporters every day. Since the deregulation of television and radio in 1996, under a plan put through by Democratic President Bill Clinton, and the auction of TV and radio frequencies to broadcasters, the Federal Communications

Commission (FCC) no longer enforces fairness rules or any semblance of what used to be known as "the fairness doctrine."

Indeed, the FCC and the Federal Government seem powerless to regulate the lies and disinformation which, in the case of the pro-Trump media machine, feeds Trump supporters and Republicans a steady diet of anti-Democratic propaganda and lies, upholding and propagating further the Big Lie that Trump won the election and that Biden stole it.

The Big Lie myth is vaguely analogous to the "Stab-in-the-back" (*"Dolchstoss"*) myth Hitler and the Nazis spread in the 1920s and early 1930s in their drive to take power, which was ultimately successful in 1933. The "Dolchstoss" or "stab-in-the-back" myth spread the totally false belief that Germany had lost World War I only as the result of betrayal by civilians on the home front, especially Jews, revolutionary socialists, and other republican politicians.

After losing the election on November 3, 2020, President Trump and his co-conspirators appeared to commit many election-related crimes aimed at overturning the results of the presidential election, whether by tampering with vote counts or pressuring election officials to find fraud where none existed; or by refusing to recognize or certify voting results, which they were obligated to do under statutory procedures designed to guarantee the accuracy of vote counts and the fairness of elections.

These apparent crimes culminated in the Capitol Insurrection on January 6, 2021, and Republican votes against certification, described above, in what was a conspiracy to deny Joe Biden the presidency. They planned to do this by refusing to vote for the congressional certification of the Electoral College vote count, as provided for in the Twelfth Amendment to the Constitution.

This is the situation Democrats and other constitutionalists face in the United States today.

Detrumpification: What Can Be Done?

What can be done? What can we learn from Germany's experience?

A complete answer to these questions cannot be provided here.

However, any effective plan of detrumpification might include the following key elements:

First, public trials will be necessary to unmask the crimes of the criminals. These trials should benefit from great media attention and be televised in whole or in part, to the full extent permitted by court regulations. The effect of the Nuremberg trials on the German population in 1945-1946 was great.

Second, the detrumpification plan should proceed from the understanding that members of the cult of Trump, like members of the cult of Adolf Hitler, will not be easy to de-program. Drastic measures are likely to be required, such as the adoption of laws and regulations to take down, or at least de-fang, the pro-Trump media machine, including, in particular, Fox News.

Legislation should be adopted to this end. One measure would be to introduce tax benefits (reductions) for real news organizations who put on objective, fact-based news programs. These benefits would not be available to propaganda operations like Fox News. Objective reporting and fairness standards could be introduced under the regulations governing administration of the tax breaks.

Third, civil penalties should be adopted to sanction the deliberate or reckless dissemination of lies and disinformation. The legal norms set forth in the Supreme Court case of *New York Times v. Sullivan (1964)* and its progeny would provide the governing legal standards, to ensure that speech protected by the First Amendment is not sanctioned.

Detrumpification will not be easy.

But it is as essential for the maintenance and growth of a vibrant democracy in the United States today as denazification was for the growth of democracy in Germany after 1945.

8

September 23, 2021

A Parable of Our Time: "Our Democratic House Is on Fire!"

BACKGROUND

See Robert Kagan, "Our Constitutional Crisis Is Already Here," *Washington Post*, September 23, 2021 (3:32 p.m. EDT).[31]

Parable

There is a man running up and down the street, with his hair all frazzled and his eyes filled with terror, shouting, "The house is on fire! Our house is on fire! Our whole democratic city is on fire!"

Outside a cafe, on a bright sunny morning, a number of people sit calmly drinking their coffee. A few, but not as many as in the past, are reading their newspapers.

"Help! Help!" the screaming man implores. "Don't you know, the whole city is on fire!"

The seated individuals proceed calmly to drink their coffee and chat among themselves.

32

"Don't you know?" the wild man implores again. "The whole city is on fire!"

Different individuals respond variously.

"You exaggerate," one says. "We don't see any flames."

"The houses in the next street are on fire," the wild man rejoins.

"Don't worry," another replies. "Someone will take care of it."

"Fake news!" another shouts out, aggressively.

"What about you newspaper readers?" the wild man screams, in exasperation.

"We know," one of them replies. "But what do you expect us to do about it? Someone will take care of it."

Another newspaper reader says, "I haven't read anything about it in my newspaper or heard anything about it on television."

"Of course not, John," another cajoles. "Look at the newspapers you read and the television stations you watch."

Another man, a thoughtful-looking gentleman, declaims, "You're right. Something is going on. We ought to launch an investigation to see who started the fire."

A teenager, sitting with her parents at the cafe, leaps to her feet and shouts out, "We know who started the fire, and who the arsonists are who have been pouring gasoline on it!"

"In this town," the wild man screams, "we have a volunteer fire department. You are all members of our volunteer fire department."

"Don't get so excited," a senior member of the group rejoins. "Someone will take care of it."

"The alarm bell at the fire department hasn't even rung," says another.

"Who disarmed the bell?" the teenager shouts out and is ignored.

"The wild man, with growing terror in his eyes, screams, "Our democratic town will be destroyed if we don't act to save it!"

"Go on, get out of here. You are disturbing our morning coffee," one man yells back as other coffee drinkers join in. "Yes, go on, get out of here. You're disturbing our morning coffee."

The screaming man yells, "The whole town is on fire and half of its citizens are pouring gasoline on the fire!

One might ask, "Does this parable have anything to do with current politics or democracy in America?"

One thinks of Katherine Anne Porter's brilliant novel, *Ship of Fools (1962)*—made into a movie[32] of the same name in 1965. In the final scene of the movie, the protagonist, a dwarf, is watching the other passengers get off the ship, including those who had argued vociferously in the movie in defense of Adolf Hitler and the Nazis.

Looking directly into the camera, he says. "You are thinking, what does all this have to do with us?' He then says, "Nothing." He chuckles, then laughs. Puffing on his cigar, he turns and walks out of the station. The movie ends.

Part Three

Russian Aggression in Ukraine and the Response of the West

9

May 8, 2023

Ukraine War: The Continuing Illusion of "Negotiations"

Wishful thinking and potential appeasement in Ukraine

Adapted rom The Trenchant Observer, May 8, 2023

Bojan Pancevski, Laurence Norman, and Vivian Salama of the Wall Street Journal report that U.S. National Security Officials (i.e., Jake Sullivan, the National Security Adviser) are now receptive to China helping to mediate a ceasefire agreement in Ukraine.1 Certain European leaders reportedly share this view (unnamed, but probably French and German).

NSC and some European officials are responding to the fact that as the war drags out, they are uncertain as to whether support for Ukraine from the West can be maintained at current levels. The Journal notes,

The supply of ammunition is a key problem because Western industrial capacity has proven unable to meet its own demands while supporting Ukraine, several officials and industry leaders said.

The reporters are talking about current "Western industrial capacity"—without moving to an emergency war production economy.

Assuming Ukraine makes significant gains in its upcoming counter-offensive, so the thinking goes, President Biden is likely to suggest to Volodymyr Zelenski that now would be a good time for negotiations.

The Journal reports further that the White House is thinking Ukraine may have to make territorial concessions. Pancevski, Norman, and Salama write,

The aim is for Ukraine to regain important territory in the south, a development that could be interpreted as a success even if Russia retains chunks of territory its forces have occupied.

"The military aid dispatched to Ukraine is designed to put Kyiv in a stronger negotiating position," the Journal reports.

Pancevski, Norman, and Salama note,

The interest in negotiations brings Washington in closer alignment with some European countries, which are eager to see the conflict end, or at the very least moderate in intensity, and have been the most intent on discussing some resolution this year.

The White House clings to the illusion of a negotiated ceasefire or settlement to the war. A resolution this year would certainly help President Joe Biden in his campaign for re-election in 2024.

Yet it is all wishful thinking. It ignores basic realities.

Ukraine is not likely to willingly accept any territorial concessions.

Such concessions would greatly undermine the norms of international law and the U.N. Charter which prohibit the international use of force and the recognition of any territorial gains achieved by military conquest. Non-recognition of such gains has been the official policy of the United since 1932 under the Stimson Doctrine. That doctrine is now embodied in peremptory norms of international law (*jus cogens*), from which there can be no exception, ***not even by agreement***.

The law of the Charter and international law governing the use of force is of critical importance in maintaining international peace and security. Any abandonment of its basic peremptory norms could lead to wars of aggression in a number of places in the world, including Taiwan.

The article by Pancevski, Norman, and Salama also reveals a fundamental flaw in U.S. strategy toward the Ukraine: a failure to understand what is really at stake in the war, and a consequent failure to take emergency actions, such as the sufficient production of munitions, that are required—for Ukraine, the West, and the U.N. Charter-based international legal order to prevail.

Biden has not yet accepted the goal of victory in this struggle, with victory being defined as Russian withdrawal of its troops from all of Ukraine together with a cessation of missile and drone attacks on Ukrainian targets, and reparations. In other words, an outcome consistent with international law, and the U.N. General Assembly Resolution adopted on February 23, 2023.

Officials like Jake Sullivan are used to resolving differences within Washington with clever words. That will not work in Ukraine.

Biden, Sullivan, and Anthony Blinken may think they can muddle through the challenge of the Ukraine War.

Yet they may be mistaken, as they were on the Afghanistan withdrawal decision.

They could lose the 2024 presidential election, particularly if the Republicans end up with a candidate other than Donald Trump.

A Republican victory in 2024 would in all likelihood be a victory for Vladimir Putin and Russia.

1 Bojan Pancevski (Berlin), Laurence Norman (Berlin), and Vivian Salama (Washington), "U.S. and Allies Look at Potential China Role in Ending Ukraine War; An expected offensive by Ukraine is seen as paving way for negotiations with Russia," Wall Street Journal, updated May 7, 2023 (2:45 pm ET).[33]

FURTHER READING ,

James Rowles, "Sudan: An inspiring story of two student taxicab heroes amidst the fighting," The Trenchant Observer, May 5, 2023.[34]

10

May 13, 2023

Ukraine: "Territorial Concessions"

Peremptory Norms of International Law
and the History of U.S. Policy

Adapted from The Trenchant Observer, May 12, 2023.[35]

The White House persists in its belief that negotiations can lead to a ceasefire or settlement in the foreseeable future.

Edward Wong and Michael Crowley, writing in the New York Times,[36] quote Secretary of State Antony Blinken as follows:

Mr. Blinken said on Tuesday at a news conference with James Cleverly, the British foreign secretary, that the Ukrainians have "what they need to continue to be successful in regaining territory that was seized by force by Russia over the last 14 months"

This statement suggests the White House does not support the expulsion of Russian troops from *all* Ukrainian territory and imagines that negotiations can lead to a ceasefire that leaves Russia in possession of the Crimea and the parts of the Donbas they brought under their control through their invasion in 2014.

President Biden and his foreign policy team obviously don't take seriously the arguments based on international law and the U.N. Charter that we have repeatedly set forth.[37] In fact, it's not even clear that they have heard them.

40

What this means is that the U.S. is driving a policy which either 1) has no chance of success, or 2) if implemented would have a disastrous impact on the ability of the U.N. Charter and international law to deter and end wars of aggression, including a potential Chinese invasion of Taiwan.

The peremptory norms of international law and the U.N. Charter (*jus cogens*) of particular relevance here are:

1   the prohibition of the threat or use of force against the territorial integrity or political independence of any state,[38]
2) the principle that any international agreement secured by coercion of a state by the threat or use of force is void,[39] and
3) the principle of non-recognition of any territorial gains achieved by military force.[40]

U.S. policymakers and leaders of other nations owe their citizens and the government and citizens of Ukraine a public explanation of how these norms apply to any ceasefire or settlement terms, and what the consequences for international peace and security would be of any agreement with Russia that ignores them.

These are norms of peremptory international law or *jus cogens*, from which there can be no derogation, not even by agreement.

Article 52 of the Vienna Convention on the Law of Treaties provides:

Article 52. *Coercion of a state by the threat or use of force*

A treaty is void if its conclusion has been procured by the threat or use of force in violation of the principles of international law embodied in the Charter of the United Nations.

Under the Vienna Convention, a "treaty" is any international agreement in written form intended to be governed by international law.

A norm of peremptory international law is defined in Art. 53 of the Vienna Convention as follows:

Article 53. *Treaties conflicting with a peremptory norm of general international law (jus cogens)*

A treaty is void if, at the time of its conclusion, it conflicts with a peremptory norm of general international law. For the purposes of the present Convention, a peremptory norm of general international law is a norm accepted and recognized by the international community of States as a whole as a norm from which no derogation is permitted and which can be modified only by a subsequent norm of international law having the same character.

Regarding the non-recognition of territorial gains achieved by the use of force, the 1970 U.N. General Assembly Declaration on Friendly Relations, which is generally accepted as an authentic interpretation of the Charter, provides:

The territory of a State shall not be the object of acquisition by another State resulting from the threat or use of force. No territorial acquisition resulting from the threat or use of force shall be recognized as legal…

The non-recognition doctrine has been U.S. policy since the Stimson Doctrine was adopted in 1932. The U.S. and the Latin American States codified this principle in Article 11 of the 1933 Montevideo Convention on the Rights and Duties of States.[41]
The Montevideo Convention was the product of Franklin D. Roosevelt's Good Neighbor Policy, which signaled an end--at least under

Roosevelt and Truman--to U.S. military interventions in the Latin American region. It was a period in which the U.S. and the Latin American States assumed a leadership role in the development of international law in general and specifically the international law of non-intervention.[42]

This same principle of non-recognition is restated in Article 21 of the 1948 Charter of the Organization of American States.[43]

What this means is that any ceasefire or peace settlement which violates the above norms of peremptory international law will be void under international law even if Russia, Ukraine, the U.S. and other NATO countries are parties to the agreement.

Any such ceasefire or settlement would be legally void and consequently unstable, and could depend only on parties acting on a political basis to enforce its provisions.

President Joe Biden and his foreign policy team, including in particular Secretary of State Antony Blinken, need to be briefed and to take into account the international law considerations outlined above.

There is really no excuse for their pushing policies that do not take peremptory norms of international law into account.

Moreover, as noted above, the legal principle of non-recognition of territories acquired by military force has been espoused and upheld by the United States for over 90 years. Significantly, the United States never recognized the Soviet military conquest and annexation in 1940 of the Baltic countries of Estonia, Latvia, and Lithuania.

Journalists, for their part, should insist on U.S. and other officials answering hard questions based on the considerations set forth above in any discussion of possible negotiations and possible terms of a ceasefire or permanent settlement in the Ukraine war.

FURTHER READING

James Rowles, "Ukraine War, May 11, 2023: Britain sends long-range missiles to Ukraine; U.S. says South Africa sends arms to Russia; Extraordinary video of Russian soldier pleading for mercy, and being escorted by drone to point of safe surrender," The Trenchant Observer, May 11, 2023.[44]

11

July 22, 2023

The Fateful Grip of War on Human Minds

Without the Goal of Peace, Peace Will Not Be Achieved

War has such a powerful grip on our minds that no one seems to be able to dream of peace.

This was not always the case. At various times throughout history, men and women have dreamed of peace, and worked hard to achieve peace.

At the First Hague Peace Conference in 1899, delegates pursuing the goal of peace sought to establish a World court to settle differences between countries not by war but rather by international adjudication and arbitration, using international law. They failed to establish a world court then, but did succeed in creating the Permanent Court of Arbitration (PCA), where it was hoped countries would submit their disputes to international arbitration.

After its creation in 1899 and its strengthening at the Second Hague Peace Conference in 1907, with funding from Andrew Carnegie a Peace Palace was built between 1907 and 1913 to house the PCA. Today, it is the home of the PCA, the International Court of Justice (ICJ) , the Hague Academy of International Law, and the Peace Palace Library.

The Permanent Court of Arbitration has proven useful over the years in resolving disputes between states, though it has been largely eclipsed by the International Court of Justice and its jurisprudence (case law).

Nonetheless, the Permanent Court of Arbitration still exists, and sometimes oversees important arbitral decisions.

In 2016, for example, in *The South China Sea Arbitration*, in proceedings conducted pursuant to provisions of the 1982 Law of the Sea Convention, an arbitral panel appointed by and operating under the rules of the Permanent Court of Arbitration rejected all of China's claims in the South China Sea, finding that none of them were supported by international law. China did not participate in the proceedings, but is bound by the decision under the terms of the Law of the Sea Convention, to which it is a party.

After the First World War, (known then as "The Great War" and also as "the war to end all wars"), the Covenant of the League of Nations was adopted at the Versailles Peace Conference in 1919. The Covenant had as its overriding goal international peace, and to that end established the Permanent Court of International Justice (PCIJ), or "World Court".

As noted above, setting up a "world court" had been a chief goal of many at the Hague Peace Conferences of 1899 and 1907. Yet only after the horrendous devastation of World War I was it finally established. The PCIJ was the predecessor of the present International Court of Justice (ICJ), established by the U.N. Charter in 1945 after the horrors of World War II.

Actually it might be more accurate to speak of the "rededication" of the World Court, as with only minor changes the Statute of the ICJ repeats verbatim the language of the Statute of the PCIJ, and the ICJ has followed and built upon the jurisprudence of the PCIJ.

The goal of peace remained a priority for the principal nations of the world in the 1920's. In 1928, they adopted a General Treaty for Renunciation of War as an Instrument of National Policy, popularly known as the Kellogg-Briand Pact or the Peace of Paris. Article I provides the following:

Article I:

> The High Contracting Parties solemnly declare in the names of their respective peoples that they condemn recourse to war for the solution of international controversies, and renounce it, as an instrument of national policy in their relations with one another.

In the 95 years since the Kellogg-Briand Pact, what has happened to the pursuit of peace which it embodied?

Adolf Hitler challenged international law and the international legal order based on the League of Nations Covenant and the Kellogg-Briand Pact by annexing Austria under the threat of invasion in March 1938, by securing the cession of the Sudetenland (German-speaking provinces) of Czechoslovakia through the infamous Munich Pact and direct military threats against Czechoslovakia in September 1938, by the invasion of the rest of Czechoslovakia in March 1939, and by the invasion of Poland on September 1, 1939, setting off the Second World War. In the ensuing months, Hitler invaded Denmark, Norway, The Netherlands, Belgium, France, and other countries.

After the war, the nations of the world met in San Francisco and adopted the United Nations Charter, which had as its principal and overriding goal the establishment and maintenance of international peace and security.

In 2008 Russia invaded Georgia, violating the Charter's prohibition of the international use of force. In 2014 it invaded Ukraine, seizing and annexing the Crimea in February and March. The West reacted with minimal sanctions which amounted to a mere slap on the wrist. Beginning in April and throughout the summer, Russia invaded the provinces of Luhansk and Donetsk in an eastern industrial region known as the Donbas.

On February 24, 2022, Russia launched an all-out invasion against all of Ukraine, in a war which continues today and shows no sign of an early end.

To be sure, the United States violated the U.N. Charter when it invaded Iraq in 2003. We and others sharply criticized this action at the time. However misguided, the U.S. invasion was never meant to be permanent, and the U.S. never sought to annex Iraqi territory.

That said, we must resist "what about" arguments if we are to succeed in establishing and maintaining international peace and security. An analogy may drive home this essential point. Domestically, the fact that individuals may have committed murders in the past is no argument against establishing the rule of law and effective deterrence and punishment of murders going forward.

Today, where in our consciousness is the goal of peace?

Generals ask for more and newer and better weapons, both to assist Ukraine and to prepare for future wars. This is not unreasonable in view of the Russian aggression in Ukraine and Chinese threats to invade Taiwan. Nonetheless, their thinking and that of their civilian leaders seems to be constrained within a paradigm of war and fighting wars.

But what has happened to the overarching goal of peace?

Is it not possible to arm and fight aggression, both present and potential, while still taking concrete actions in pursuit of the goal of peace?

During World War II the West had extraordinary leaders in the persons of Franklin Roosevelt and Winston Churchill and their associates. They were clear in their minds that while they were fighting to defeat Germany and Japan, to be sure, they were at the same time fighting to establish peace and an international legal order with institutions that might act effectively to maintain the peace.

Today we see very little of the clarity of mind Roosevelt and Churchill had regarding the need to establish or strengthen institutions charged with the maintenance of international peace and security.

The dream of peace seems to have given way to resignation to the fact that the world will always be in or on the verge of a state of war.

This is a mind-boggling statement....

This is a mind-boggling statement, given the realities of current nuclear weapons states capable of destroying mankind many times over, and the prospects of an accelerating spread of nuclear weapons. After the Covid pandemic, we must also be thinking of the risks of new biological weapons devised with all the tools of genetic engineering, of the risks of new weapons of unimaginable power and destructiveness driven by artificial intelligence, and of the risks of new forms of international conflict which may emerge as a consequence of global warming and the attendant mass migrations of tens or hundreds of millions of people.

The United Nations was devised in 1945 and has grown in capacity since as the principal tool of humanity for managing its common affairs.

That tool is a creation of international law. Effective use of the tool by humanity to manage its affairs depends on the effective use of international law, within the framework of the U.N. Charter or what might be termed the Constitution of World Society. (The name in French of the League of Nations was *La Société des Nations*.)

It is the only tool with the capacity or potential to coordinate the affairs of some eight billion members of humanity, and to defend their interests such as their physical survival on a rapidly warming planet.

If we think of things in this all-encompassing way, we can begin to understand that the United Nations and its key institutions are, in effect, the brain of humanity. It is humanity's most important organ because it alone can mobilize and coordinate the actions of humanity's eight billion members.

From this perspective we can now appreciate that the goal of peace is intricately related to the goal of humanity's survival.

We must now understand that Vladimir Putin's war against Ukraine, international law, the United Nations Charter, and the United Nations itself, is an attack on humanity's brain.

It is an attack on the only organ capable of mobilizing and coordinating the energies and actions of the eight billion inhabitants of this planet.

To stop global warming, before it stops us.

To control the power of artificial intelligence, before it controls us.

To control nuclear proliferation and limit nuclear weapons, before "limited" nuclear wars escalate to wars that end human life on this planet.

To prevent and control the development and deployment of increasingly powerful weapons of mass destruction aided by the relentless advance of science and technology.

While few leaders may have thought in precisely these terms in the past, they must do so now.

Putin's and Russia's attack on humanity's brain must be repulsed.

Putin and Russia must be defeated, as must any other country which launches a similar assault on international law, the U.N. Charter, and the United Nations itself—which together constitute humanity's brain.

For without humanity's brain, we are all lost.

12

August 3, 2023

When Reason is Swept Aside

Remembering Adolf Hitler and Nazi Germany

Even before Jack Smith announced the indictment of Donald Trump for his role in the attempted coup d'état in 2021, I was thinking of the first half of the twentieth century, when mass political emotions overwhelmed reason and democracy in Italy, Germany, and other countries.

It seems today that those who oppose the fascist movement in the United States led by Donald Trump and his acolytes in the Republican party are placing most of their bets on the triumph of reason, in the belief that people are essentially guided by reason, and that no reasonable man or woman could vote for Donald Trump, a former president now indicted for trying to overthrow the Constitution and the democratic government of the United States.

See Maureen Dowd, "Coup-Coup-Ca-Choo, Trump-Style," New York Times, August 5, 2023.[45]

Yet stranger things have happened. Germany provides the most obvious and provocative example.

One should perhaps reread and study carefully the classic text by José Ortega y Gasset (*The Revolt of the Masses*, 1930), who identified the profound changes taking place in the European mass psyche, to better understand how the power of Unreason grew to such an extent that it overpowered Reason itself, leading to such gruesome events as those of World War II and the extermination of the Jews, the gypsies, and otters deemed unworthy of life.

Given the horrendous things that were going on in the Soviet Union after the Bolsheviks' 1917 October Revolution, and the deep misgivings about the power of Reason after the incredibly irrational, stupid, and destructive war of 1914-1918, public opinion in Europe was subject to irrational mass emotions skillfully manipulated by political leaders.

Adolf Hitler's Nazi Party never received more than 37.3% of the popular votes in free elections.

That is roughly the number of Trump's hard-core supporters, by way of comparison. A recent poll showed that Biden and Trump are essentially tied in the race for the presidency in 2024. Another point of comparison.

Hitler achieved his level of support, which led to the Nazi Party emerging with the largest number of seats in ahe Reichstag (German parliament), in both the July and the November 1932 elections, with 37.3% and 33.1% of the popular vote, respectively.

Even in the March 5, 1933 elections which were not free, the Nazi Party did not gain a majority, receiving only 43.91% of the vote. These elections took place after the Reichstag fire and during the harsh repression and arrests of Communists and other opposition leaders.

After his failed beer hall Putsch in Munich in 1923 and while in prison writing *Mein Kampf* ("My Struggle"), his political screed, Hitler had made no secret of his violent and hate-filled sentiments against Jews and other defenders of the democratic order based on reason and democratic precepts.

One needs only to listen to Hitler's speeches in German, as I have done, or in German with subtitles as anyone can do, to understand the hate and vile statements they contained.

You have to listen to these speeches in German, even with subtitles, to understand their effect on people. There was something mesmerizing about them, some kind of primal scream, which bypassing the brains of those in Hitler's audiences penetrated to the depths of their psyches and hearts.

And yet it was that very hate and violent rhetoric which drew his supporters to him. In the April 10, 1932 run-off elections for the presidency, incumbent President Paul von Hindenburg won 53% of the vote, Hitler, 36.8%, and the Communist candidate 10.2%.

In the July 1932 Reichstag elections, the Nazi Party won 37.3% of the vote and was easily the largest party in the Reichstag. Significantly, except for the Catholics, the middle and upper classes had gone over to the Nazis.

Could it happen here?

See Sinclair Lewis' humorous but insightful novel, *It Can't Happen Here* (1935).

Of course, one might pose the question differently, e.g., "Is there any reason it can't happen here?"

Recommended reading for all concerned citizens:

William L. Shirer, *The Rise and Fall of the Third Reich: A History of Nazi Germany* (Simon and Shuster, 1960), The 50th anniversary edition is a beautifully produced book, 1147 pp. of text plus Introduction and footnotes.

In a country in which half the electorate, or at least 35-40% of the electorate, don't have an accurate understanding of essential political facts, or say they don't care if the former President while in office tried to overthrow the election and the Constitution, we are in uncharted waters.

This is the world we are living in, today, in the United States.

We are in extremely dangerous waters, where an unpredictable wave of mass emotions could overturn our democratic ship of state.

The battle to save our democracy may not be decided by voters following reason.

It is important to continue to convince and motivate those who *are* guided by reason. But it is also important, and perhaps even more important, to undertake actions that might sway those who are not currently listening to reason.

Massive campaigns should be launched now to help shape political debate and the electoral battlefield.

How to do that should be an overriding focus of concern.

FURTHER READING

1)"Sleepwalking in the garden of fascism: 'Merrily we roll along!'" The Trenchant Observer, June 2, 2021.[46]

2)"A Parable of our time: "Our democratic house is on fire!" The Trenchant Observer, September 23, 2021.[47]

13

August 9, 2023

Roger Cohen on
"Putin's Forever War"

BAKGROUND

See,

Roger Cohen, "Putin's Forever War, New York Times, August 6, 2023.[48]

New York Times Paris Bureau Chief reports on a month-long trip in Russia

We have long advanced the view that the Russian war of aggression against Ukraine is a civilizational struggle[49] We have also commented on parallels between Vladimir Putin's Russia and Adolf Hitler's Germany[50] Roger Cohen, the former long-time columnist of the New York Times and its current bureau chief in Paris, in a magisterial article[51] offers keen insights into Russian support for the war and Vladimir Putin's view and goal of a civilizational struggle against the West.

To understand Russian support for the war and the reasons it is likely to continue for years into the future, concerned readers could do no better than to read Cohen's long article in its entirety.

55

Cohen sees Putin as secure in his power and control over the country he rules. Relentless state propaganda, particularly on TV, and the indoctrination of younger generations remind one of the hold over the population of Germany that Adolf Hitler and his propaganda minister Josef Goebbels developed and maintained throughout the 1930's and World War II.

To be sure, many younger citizens take a more critical view of the war and Putin's regime. But they do not constitute a force that could threaten Putin's hold on power. Dissent is vigorously suppressed.

Reading Cohen's article, one cannot escape the conclusion that the Ukrainian war may continue for a very long time, and that the risk of defeat for Ukraine by the country that defeated Nazi Germany on the eastern front in World War II will remain large and ever-present for as long as the war lasts.

14

August 21, 2023

Ukraine and the Republican Debate on Wednesday, August 23

The most fateful questions may not be asked or debated at the Republican televised debate on Wednesday, August 23. The debate will be broadcast on Fox News from 9-11 pm ET.

Those questions relate to the policy of the different candidates toward continuing to provide military and economic support to Ukraine, to meet the requirements of Ukraine, and continued leadership of the Western alliance supporting Ukraine with weapons and money.

In the United States, we are living in a news silo in which the cable news media are obsessed with the details of the criminal legal proceedings against Donald Trump, as if they were presenting an ongoing series of CSI-style crime dramas.

Today there is little coverage of world affairs. Coverage of the Ukraine war seems limited to the latest "breaking news". As a result, viewers may have little interest in the Ukraine war, and consequently the cable news channels, driven by the quest for ratings and profit, may pay little attention to **the gravest challenge facing America today:**

How will the U.S. respond going forward to the challenges represented by continuing Russian aggression against Ukraine, and the

continuing commission of war crimes, crimes against humanity, and acts of genocide against its population?

Donald Trump and most but not all of the candidates for the Republican nomination have taken positions indicating they would not continue such support.[52]

In view of the above, the key issues that should be debated on Wednesday include the following:

1) Will a candidate condemn tbe Russian invasion of Ukraine and vow to continue military and economic assistance to Ukraine at levels that are needed, and will he or she pledge to uphold the sanctions in place against Russia?
2) What does the candidate believe should be done, if anything, to uphold international law and the United Nations Charter, and the current U.N.Charter-based international order?
3) What relationship does the candidate see between the war in Ukraine and the ability of the world's nations acting through the United Nations to meet the challenges of global warming and climate change?

Candidates should be required to state what specific actions they would take to implement the policies they say they would support.

As when Britain and the West faced Nazi Germany in 1940 and throughout World War II, the United States and the West today face historical challenges which will decide whether tens or hundreds of millions of people live in freedom or under totalitarian dictatorships.

On which side will America stand if a particular candidate becomes President of the United States?

That is a question worthy of debate, especially at the Republican debate among primary candidates on Wednesday night.

FURTHER READING

1) "REPRISE (from January 26, 2022): Reflections on Czechoslovakia (1968) and Ukraine (2022)-- August 20, 1968: 'Dubček, Svoboda!'", The Trenchant Observer, August 21, 2023.[53]

2) "Ukraine War, August 17, 2023: *Le Monde* editorial highlights strategic failures of the West," The Trenchant Observer, August 17, 2023.[54]

15

August 31, 2023

The Decline of Truth and Respect for Expertise

The Foreign Policy Ignorance of the American Electorate and its Portents

Civil ignorance is not new, but the abandonment of truth by part of the political class may be.

The Republican debate on Wednesday night, August 23, 2023, brought home a few deeply-troubling realities.

Swarmy Vivek Ramaswamy, parroting Donald Trump, argued we should cut our aid to Ukraine, and devote our resources to defending our southern border from the "invasion" of aliens and asylum seekers who are entering the U.S.

Nikki Haley called him out for wanting to hand Ukraine to Vladimir Putin, and surrender Taiwan to China. **"You have no foreign policy experience and it shows,"** she declared, as she took down Ramaswamy and showed the world there is no substance beneath the glib millionaire's patter. Ramaswamy has no government experience or any other qualifications to be president.

Why is he in the race? Could Trump donors be supporting other candidates just to divide the field and ensure support does not coalesce around a single challenger to Trump? Being rich is not a sufficient qualification to be president.

Thirty years ago, a candidate like Ramaswamy would never have made it onto the debate stage.

Behind Haley's putdown lies another even more troubling truth.

The Republican Party and its Trump supporters have no memory of history, no understanding of government or international affairs, and are not shocked by what Ramaswamy said about supporting Ukraine, ... OR... Or Trump supporters who, like many of those in leadership positions, have sacrificed honor and truth in the service of personal ambition.

As David French points out in an insightful Washington Post opinion column[55] civic ignorance is not new. What is new is the attitude and actions of a large portion of the political class. This explains the current crisis America faces.

French writes about "the specific way in which poor leadership transforms civic ignorance from a problem into a crisis — a crisis that can have catastrophic effects on the nation and, ultimately, the world." He continues,

Civic ignorance is a very old American problem. If you spend five seconds researching what Americans know about their own history and their own government, you'll uncover an avalanche of troubling research, much of it dating back decades. As Samuel Goldman detailed two years ago, as far back as 1943, 77 percent of Americans knew essentially nothing about the Bill of Rights, and in

1952 only 19 percent could name the three branches of government.

Civic ignorance in general is not new, and foreign policy ignorance is even greater. What is different is that political elites used to compensate for this ignorance, but significant portions of them no longer do so. French explains,

Simply put, civic ignorance was a serious but manageable problem, as long as our leader class and key institutions still broadly, if imperfectly, cared about truth and knowledge — and as long as our citizens cared about the opinions of that leader class and those institutions.

French comments on Ramaswamy's ignorant or cynical use of statements that have no basis in truth. Given his educational background (Harvard College and Yale Law School), the "ignorant" explanation is extremely unlikely. He is a smart, cynical politician who appears to deliberately and knowingly lie in the service of his own political ambition, He is emblematic of a whole class of politicians who have placed American democracy in peril.

French continues,

The bottom line is this: When a political class still broadly believes in policing dishonesty, the nation can manage the negative effects of widespread civic ignorance. When the political class corrects itself, the people will tend to follow.

But when key members of the political class abandon any pretense of knowledge or truth, a poorly informed public is simply unequipped to hold them to account.

And when you combine ignorance with unrelenting partisan hostility, the challenge grows all the greater. After all, it's not as though members of the political class didn't try to challenge Trump. But since that challenge came mostly from people Trump supporters loathe, such as Democratic politicians, members of the media and a few Trump-skeptical or Never Trump writers and politicians, their minds were closed. Because of the enormous amount of public ignorance, voters often didn't know that Trump was lying or making fantastically unrealistic promises, and they shut out every voice that could tell them the truth.

A democracy needs an informed public and a basically honest political class. It can muddle through without one or the other, but when it loses both, the democratic experiment is in peril. A public that knows little except that it despises its opponents will be vulnerable to even the most bizarre conspiracy theories, as we saw after the 2020 election. And when leaders ruthlessly exploit that ignorance and animosity, the Republic can fracture. How long can we endure the consequences of millions of Americans believing the most fantastical lies?

30-40% of the electorate, or more, are ignorant or cynical and support such irresponsible positions as those Ramaswamy and Trump have put forth regarding support for Ukraine.

Let us recall. Donald Trump has never criticized Vladimir Putin. Not once. He is, in fact, Putin's Trojan Horse, and Russia's best hope for an early victory in the Ukraine war.

The problem with an ignorant electorate is that political debates become circus shouting matches, where serious consideration of fateful issues yields to spectacle.

As Timothy Snyder pointed out in his classic primer, *On Tyranny* (2017), once you have destroyed the concept of truth, as Trump has done with his cult followers, all that is left is spectacle, where "the biggest wallet pays for the most blinding lights" (Chapter 10).

When truth has been vanquished, expertise is no longer valued.

What we are left with, as we were Wednesday night, is a lot of bickering and grandstanding at the third-grade level. Those few who made serious, rational arguments were immediately dismissed by journalists (viewing the candidates' pre-debate poll numbers) as having little or no chance of winning the nomination.

It is incredibly hard to conduct a rational debate before a highly agitated and ignorant crowd, even if that crowd is the entire Republican Party.

If only for the benefit of those whose minds are not hermetically closed, what is needed are little history and civic lessons accompanying every statement of a position. What is international law? What is the United Nations Charter? Why is its prohibition of the use of force across international frontiers so important? What were the lessons of World War II? Why are international human rights important? What did we learn from Hitler and the Nazis about human rights?

It is even possible that the accumulation pf such factual explanations could have an impact on Trump cult followers. Cult experts suggest this is s the path some cult members follow in gradually breaking free of the cult's grip on their minds.[56]

The Democrats certainly have their work cut out for them in trying to explain history, World War II, and international relations to an ignorant electorate.

But they absolutely must try, every time they take a position.

In short, they have to lead.

I know that is asking a lot from the Democrats, or any politician, in 2023. But it is urgently required.

Haley might just as well have said, to the entire country, "You have no foreign policy knowledge or memory and it shows."

Unfortunately this foreign-policy ignorance could have disastrous consequences for the whole world.

Without foreign policy experts who are respected by political leaders and the population, without the concepts of honor and truth, anything can happen in the 2024 elections.

See also "Ukraine War, August 26, 2023: Republican unity and the fascist threat," The Trenchant Observer, August 26, 2023.[57]

16

September 7, 2023

Biden's Withdrawal from Afghanistan Could Cost Him the Election

Franklin Foer, a writer for *The Atlantic*, has published excerpts from his forthcoming book, *The Last Politician: Inside Joe Biden's White House and the Struggle for America's Future.*[58] The excerpts from the book constitute a one-sided and uncritical account of the American withdrawal from Afghanistan and evacuation from Kabul in August, 2021.

The excerpts from the book constitute the equivalent of a gushing one-sided eyewitness news report.

Devoid of political or strategic insight, the book is essentially an apology for the good intentions and difficult emotions experienced by American officials as they saw the catastrophic and entirely predictable effects of President Joe Biden's calamitous decision in April 2021 to withdraw *all* American troops and contractors from the country.

While the experiences of specific Afghanis is not described in any detail, the author does note the anguish felt by State Department officials including those working on a Task Force dealing with the evacuation. Foer reports as follows:

When Wendy Sherman, the deputy secretary of state, went to check in with members of a task force working on the evacuation, she found grizzled diplomats in tears. She estimated that a quarter of the State Department's personnel had served in Afghanistan. They felt a connection with the country, an emotional entanglement. Fielding an overwhelming volume of emails describing hardship cases, they easily imagined the faces of refugees. They felt the shame and anger that come with the inability to help. ***To deal with the trauma, the State Department procured therapy dogs that might ease the staff's pain (emphasis added).***

The book is deeply offensive, uncritically portraying as it does the hubris and self-centered nature of America's involvement in Afghanistan.

On the other hand, it provides interesting details about what was going through American officials' minds during the withdrawal and evacuation of Kabul in August 2021.

Ultimately, the book underlines the fundamental shortcomings of a book based on numerous interviews with key participants in events, and little else.

This is journalism, but not journalism at its best, and not journalism as the first draft of history.

In contrast to Foer, Marc A. Thiessen, a pro-Republican columnist for the Washington Post, has put together a devastating analysis of President Joe Biden's withdrawal from Afghanistan, its impact on public opinion, and how it could cost him the election in 2024.[59]

Thiessen succinctly analyzes the misrepresentations and simple lies by Biden regarding support for his decision among military leaders and other aspects of the withdrawal, including his affirmation that the withdrawal from Afghanistan was "an extraordinary success".

We have spoken out about the incompetence of Biden's foreign policy team, and repeatedly urged that it be strengthened and that key figures be replaced.

We have characterized the Afghanistan withdrawal decision as the most catastrophic foreign policy decision by a Western leader since Èdouard Daladier and Neville Chamberlain agreed to cede the Sudetenland to Adolf Hitler in the infamous 1938 Munich Pact.

A very strong case can be made that Biden's decision to withdraw from Afghanistan in April 2021, his summit meeting with Vladimir Putin in June, and the disastrous execution of the withdrawal in July and August, emboldened Putin to invade Ukraine on February 24, 2022.

In March 2021 Russia was massing troops for an invasion of Ukraine. In April, Biden decided to withdraw from Afghanistan and Russia stopped threatening an invasion. Whether there was a connection between the two developments is not publicly known. In June, Putin and Biden met in person. The chaotic withdrawal from Afghanistan culminated in August 2021. By October, Putin was planning a renewed invasion of Ukraine, which Russia first invaded in 2014.

Biden's disastrous foreign policy judgment and decisions could cost the Democrats the presidency in 2024.

From an objective point of view, he is not a viable candidate for the 2024 election. His poll numbers are disastrous and point to a Democratic loss if he is the candidate. His and the Democrats' best chance of victory is if Donald Trump is the Republican candidate in November 2024.

FURTHER READING,

1) James Rowles, "Ukraine War, September 11, 2023: Biden's failed foreign policy leadership--The West, and the Global South," The Trenchant Observer, September 11, 2023.[60]

2) James Rowles, "Ukraine war, September 9, 2023: Bankruptcy of Biden's foreign policy revealed in G-20 Communique in New Delhi," The Trenchant Observer, September 9, 2023.[61]

Part Four

The Banana Republican Party and the American Political Circus

17

September 12, 2023

The American Political Circus:

The "Banana Republic" Republicans Want to Impeach Joe Biden

La promptitude à croire le mal sans l'avoir assez examiné est un effet de l'orgueil et de la paresse. On veut trouver des coupables; et on ne veut pas se d'donner la peine d'examiner les crimes.
—La Rochefoucauld (1613-1680*), Maximes et Réflections Diverses* (Maxime 267)

(English translation (by the author)

The readiness to believe in evil without having sufficiently investigated it is an effect of pride and laziness. One wants to find the guilty, but one doesn't want to take the trouble to investigate the crimes.

We as a nation lack the candor to discuss in forthright terms what the performers in the Republican circus are doing with their power these days.

They have become vibrant examples of the *opera buffa* clowns who have populated so-called "banana republics" in the past.

La Rochefoucauld in his Maxim No. 267 refers to those who zealously seek out the guilty without taking the trouble to investigate their crimes.

This is what happened in the Spanish Inquisition, and what happens today in many dictatorships where there is no rule of law. One has political enemies and would like to see them condemned and put in prison for their crimes. Of course, there is no impartial and fair investigation into whether they have in fact committed any crimes.

They are guilty, so they must have committed crimes. So the thinking goes.

That is part of the thinking in the Republican Party that led House Speaker Kevin McCarthy to launch an impeachment investigation into Joe Biden today.[62]

Though vastly different, this is in essence the approach of Vladimir Putin in persecuting his political rivals such as Alexander Navalny, or critics such as Vladimir Kara-Murza, the New York Times columnist now condemned for what seems forever on trumped-up charges in Russia.

Republicans control the House of Representatives, which has the power under the Constitution to impeach a president for "high crimes and misdemeanors". The Republicans want to use that power as a weapon in their no-holds-barred war against the Democrats to gain power.

They want to go on a fishing expedition into the affairs of Hunter Biden, the president's son who has benefitted from his presumed influence with his father. After years of investigation, no evidence has emerged of any serious impropriety by the President.

There is, it should be noted, no parallel investigation being launched into whether Donald Trump's children used their father's influence to gain business advantages, and whether any of it benefitted Donald Trump. One would want to learn more about how Ivanka Trump got her trademark applications approved in China, and about Jared Kushner's dealings with Middle Eastern potentates, their investments in his or his family's properties, and whether any of this benefitted Donald Trump.

With so many other apparent crimes by Trump to investigate, this subject has largely escaped attention.

We're not talking about fairness or impartiality here, with the Republican majority in the House.

Without any evidence of wrongdoing by the President, the House Republicans are abusing their power in opening an impeachment investigation into Joe Biden.

The same kind of scenario is playing out in many parts of the country.

In Georgia Republicans have passed a law which allows the legislature to remove prosecutors, even in the middle of an ongoing case.

They want to resolve the indictments of Donald Trump and his 18 alleged co-conspirators for trying to overthrow the election and the Constitution by firing the prosecutor, just as they hope to end all federal prosecutions against Trump and his associates by winning the 2024 presidential election and securing the pardon of all involved.

This is the way law is used to persecute opponents and secure impunity for real crimes in Banana Republics.

The Republicans are in effect, and without a trace of shame, acting to turn the United States into a Banana Republic.

They might as well change their name to that of the "Banana Republican Party".

And yet, in newspapers and on television, reporters and commentators address these antics in serious tones.

This would be a hilarious *opera buffa* or comic opera if it weren't actually happening, today, in the United States.

Still, we should retain our sense of outrage and our readiness to call out the absurd. We must continue to ridicule this circus show as it unfolds.

While the clowns are transparently seeking to muddy the waters and confuse the voters with a trumped-up impeachment vote in the House, we should denounce it for what it is: a transparent abuse of power by the Banana Republican Party.

18

September 20, 2023

Lessons from the Ukraine War—On Freedom

When I read about or see on TV Republicans like House Leader Kevin McCarthy question further military aid for Ukraine, which is not in the current Republican budget proposal (or its outline), I wonder to myself what has happened to our belief in Freedom.

This core value of the old Republican Party was deeply held by Republican presidents like Ronald Reagan and George Herbert Walker Bush who oversaw the lead-up to and collapse of the Berlin Wall in 1989, and the spread of Liberty, of Freedom, to the subjugated peoples of Central and Eastern Europe who had lived under Soviet-controlled totalitarian regimes since shortly after the end of World War II.

Can we really understand and feel what it meant to the individuals in those countries to suddenly experience Freedom or its imminent promise?

Is it simply that the cult of Donald Trump has erased all Republican values such as the belief in truth, in the rules and procedures of democratic government, and in the very goal of Freedom itself?

Or is this apparent turning away from the value and goal of Freedom the product of other forces as well?

Do Republicans today, and American voters in general, have any appreciation of what is involved in living under a dictatorship where there is no Freedom?

Memories from Eastern Europe have faded, some 24 years after the Berlin Wall came down. Veterans of World War II, the Korean War, and the Vietnam War have passed or are passing from the scene, and with them memories of their own motivations and those of fallen comrades who died believing they were fighting for Freedom.

Their spouses and children who also lived through these wars and the terrible uncertainty of not knowing if their husbands or fathers would be coming home have also passed or are passing from the scene.

Memories of Augusto Pinochet's dictatorship in Chile, which began with a coup d'état 50 years ago, or that of the military junta in Argentina which was responsible for killing or "disappearing" some 30,000 innocent people have apparently disappeared from contemporary American consciousness.

And today there are so many dictatorships, including Russia and China, that it has become hard to feel any sympathy for individuals who live in countries where there is no Freedom. Our sympathies and sensibilities have become overwhelmed. We have become numb. And the response of many has been to simply look away.

To be sure, for a time Americans felt sympathy for the civilian victims of Russian aggression in Ukraine and the refugees it produced. But TV coverage has waned, and memories are short.

What is it like, not only to be a victim of gross human rights abuses as in Iran or Afghanistan or in Ukrainian territory under Russian occupation, but also just simply to live in a country where there is no rule of law and no Freedom?

Americans, some 247 years after the American Revolution, seem to take Freedom for granted.

They can express political views and organize to effect political change. They can speak freely about any subject. They can sue their government and U.S. and foreign citizens and corporations in courts that adhere to the Rule of Law.

Freedom means that students can study what they want and choose the kind of work they want to do. Americans can freely choose who they want to marry or live with and raise a family.

They can live anywhere they want. They can travel freely anywhere they like, both in the U.S. and abroad.

Freedom of thought means they can espouse any idea, and read any book. Freedom of religion means they may follow any creed.

One could write a book, as many have, on the multitudinous dimensions of liberty and Freedom, and what its absence has been like in many countries across the world and across the centuries.

We should meditate on the meaning of Freedom, and always remember what its absence has been like, in Nazi Germany, in the Soviet Union, in Eastern Europe, in Russia, in China, and in the many dictatorships that have existed and still exist in the world today.

Frankly, I can't understand how Republican leaders like Kevin McCarthy can care so little about Freedom. I can't understand the thrust of his questions about and objections to providing Ukraine with the military and economic aid it desperately needs to ensure that Freedom will prevail in that country, and beyond.

Just as the Americans bore the torch of Freedom in the wars of the twentieth century, the Ukrainians are bearing that torch now at immense personal sacrifice, not only for themselves but also for all of us.

Are we to believe that the Republican Party, in its current incarnation, doesn't care about Freedom, that it doesn't care enough about Freedom to support Ukraine's defense against Russia's military aggression and barbarism in the conduct of the war?

In the end, are we going to abandon Ukraine like we abandoned Afghanistan?

Donald Trump has never criticized Vladimir Putin. If elected in 2024, he will surely lead us down the road of appeasement.

Where will that road lead?

Will it lead to Freedom?

19

September 28, 2023

SATIRE: Impeachment–Republicans Focus on Biden's Dogs

House Republicans on the Biden impeachment panel have come up with at least one ground for impeaching President Joe Biden. The ground is that his dogs have been aggressive toward and biting Secret Service agents,[63] according to one well-placed source who must remain anonymous because he or she is not authorized to speak about such sensitive matters.

According to the source, House impeachment panel members have concluded that because Biden spends a lot of time with his dogs ("man's best friends"), the dogs have absorbed Biden's anger and aggression to such an extent that they have become his agents.

In legal terms, this means that it has been Joe Biden who has been biting the Secret Service agents. Such actions amount to the commission of the felony of battery upon a federal official. Consequently, for these "high crimes and misdemeanors" the President must be impeached.

Marisa Inti in *The Washington Post*, quoting Elizabeth Alexander, a spokeswoman for first lady Jill Biden, reports on probable arguments Biden may raise in his defense.[64] Inti quotes Alexander as follows:

As we've noted before, the White House can be a stressful environment for family pets, and the First Family continues to work on ways to help Commander handle the often-unpredictable nature of the White House grounds.

However, according to legal experts, if the dogs are acting as Biden's agents, their state of mind would be irrelevant. They are simply taking out Biden's anger and aggression by biting the Secret Service agents, and under well-established principles of agency law their bites are legally bites by the President.

Meanwhile, the impeachment panel continues its search for additional grounds of impeachment.

20

November 24, 2023

Irrational Belief in Rationality

Democrats Believing in a Rational World
Head Toward a Presidential Defeat

President Joe Biden appears increasingly unlikely to win the November 2024 election running against former President Donald Trump.

With poll results showing that Biden would lose five of the six states needed for electoral victory if the election were held today,[65] Democrats continue to support, even if passively, Joe Biden's death-grip on the Democratic nomination and the future of democracy and the rule of law in the United States.[66]

Biden seems to be an emotional and stubborn old man with an iron will to hang on to power, no matter what the risks to the Democrats and to the future of the country may be.

He could go down in history as a man who saved America from the authoritarianism of Donald Trump while achieving major legislative victories and managing the economy with excellent results. Or he could go down in history as a man who out of personal hubris and hunger for power risked both his own fate and that of the country, and lost.

From any rational point of view, there are few considerations that might justify risking it all when other, younger, Democratic candidates might have a much better chance of beating the presumptive or any other Republican candidate.

The extraordinary paradox is that this rational analysis runs counter to the almost religious belief of Democratic leaders that the outcome of the 2024 presidential election will be determined by voters acting in a world of reason.

Unfortunately, it is this unquestioned, bedrock belief that constitutes the Democrats' greatest weakness, and the greatest risk for the future of the country.

Democrats today, by and large, live in a world in which they believe that voters are rational and that the presidential election in 2024 will be determined by reason. This belief is in their DNA. In this world, the great achievements of the Biden administration on the domestic front will, when voters finally focus on the bread-and-butter issues that matter most to them, necessarily lead them to vote for Joe Biden, for the Democrats, and for the policies they support.[67] The fact that this did not occur in 2016 is simply dismissed. In this world, Biden's foreign policy record, which upon close examination is questionable at best, is assumed to have no bearing on the outcome of the election.

Democrats ignore the fact that the polls show that half the voters voice a preference for Trump, and that Republican representatives in the House and the Senate express support for Trump and even for the crazy belief that Trump won the 2020 election.

Democrats answer critiques based on Biden's (and Harris's) extremely low (and sinking?) standing in the polls with rational arguments. These low ratings, however, have been a constant since Biden's catastrophic withdrawal from Afghanistan in the summer of 2021.

They ignore the fact that politics in the U.S. is not taking place in a rational world. Consider the following analysis by Thomas B. Edsall which summarizes the negatives against Trump, who nonetheless enjoys the support of half the electorate and more than that in five of the key battleground states according to the latest polls.

See "Thomas B. Edsall, "The Roots of Trump's Rage," New York Times, November 22, 2022.[68]

Edsall quotes Brian Klass of the University College of London, who in an October 1, 2023 article wrote the following:[69]

There are now two leading candidates for the American presidency. One of them is a 77 year-old racist,[70] misogynist[71] bigot who has been found liable for rape,[72] who incited a deadly, violent insurrection aimed at overturning a democratic election, who has committed mass fraud[73] for personal enrichment, who is facing 91 separate counts of felony criminal charges[74] against him, and who has overtly discussed his authoritarian strategies[75] for governing if he returns to power.

The other is 80 years old with mainstream Democratic party views who sometimes misspeaks or trips. (There may be other reasons to criticize Joe Biden, but the main one discussed in the press is his age).

One of those two candidates faces relentless newspaper columns and TV pundit "takes" arguing that he should drop out of the race. (Spoiler alert: it's somehow *not* the racist authoritarian sexual abuse fraudster facing 91 felony charges).

Considering the above, it appears that reason is clearly not determining the preferences of half or more of the voters in states which are of decisive importance for the electoral college vote.

One is hard-pressed to avoid the conclusion that the belief of the Democrats in a rational world and that in that rational world Joe Biden can win reelection in 2024 is itself irrational.

It is irrational in that it ignores obvious facts and assumes a Biden and Democratic victory essentially on the basis of an irrational belief that voters will vote rationally in the presidential election in November 2024.

This faith in a rational world in which voters make rational choices is contradicted by abundant present and historical evidence.

Mass political emotions are sweeping through the American body politic. Democrats and all small "d" democrats need to open their eyes, grasp current realities, and act accordingly.

A rational response to the irrational world in which America currently exists would be to wrest the Democratic nomination from the death-grip of an old and stubborn man who, despite his achievements and current abilities, is widely perceived as being too old (he will be 82 weeks after the 2024 election) and lacking the abilities to be an effective president, and who is detested–irrationally–by a very large portion of the electorate.

In this irrational world of politics in America today, a Democratic candidate such as Governor Gavin Newson of California or Governor Gretchen Whitmer of Michigan would probably have a much greater chance of defeating Donald Trump or another Republican than would Joe Biden.

This fact is not rational. This fact is not fair.

But it is very real, and the nomination of Newsom or Whitmer would represent a very rational response to the irrational world in which the next president (and House and Senate) will be elected in November 2024.

FURTHER READING

1) James Rowles, "REVISED AND UPDATED: The decline of truth and respect for expertise: The foreign policy ignorance of the American electorate and its portents; Civil ignorance is not new, but the abandonment of truth by part of the political class may be.," Trenchant Observations, August 31, 2023.[76]

2) James Rowles, "When reason is swept aside: Remembering Adolf Hitler and Nazi Germany," Trenchant Observations, August 3, 2023.[77]

21

December 8, 2023

Pearl Harbor, History, and Aid for Ukraine

The America First movement in the United States was led by isolationists who believed the country should not get involved in any war in Europe. World War II was launched by Adolf Hitler when Germany invaded Poland on September 1, 1939. Germany was joined by the Soviet Union on September 17 when it invaded eastern Poland, pursuant to the Molotov-von Rippentrop Non-agression Pact concluded in August, and its secret Protocol calling for the division of Poland between the two countries.

During 1940 only Great Britain fought on, alone. Franklin D. Roosevelt wanted to help but was constrained by the isolationists in Congress. Nonetheless, he was able to secure passage of the Lend-Lease Act in March 1941, which allowed Britain to acquire military aid from the U.S. on credit, as it were. This American military assistance was a vital lifeline which enabled Britain to keep up the fight against Germany.

Nonetheless, the situation facing Prime Minister Winston Churchill and Great Britain in early December 1941 was grave. Hitler's indomitable war machine stood unchallenged on the continent of Europe, and fears of a German invasion of Britain persisted, despite Hitler's invasion of the SovietUnion in June 1941.

Churchill nurtured the hope that America would enter the war and help defeat Hitler's forces, as its entry into World War I had ensured the defeat of Germany and Austria.

Yet given the opposition of the isolationists, the America First Movement, it was not clear whether the U.S. would enter the war and if it would do so before it was too late for Britain.

Then, on December 7, 1941, Japan bombed Pearl Harbor.

Churchill was greatly relieved, because he thought Japan's war against the U.S. would bring America into the European war, while also relieving pressure on outposts of the British Empire in Asia.

During 1940 the Nazis conquered the major countries in Europe except Sweden, Switzerland, Spain and Portugal, and Germany's ally Italy.

Churchill later said that the Allies' secret weapon in World War II was the military genius of Corporal Schickengruber (a derogatory reference to Adolf Hitler using his grandfather's last name).

Corporal Schickengruber showed his genius four days after Pearl Harbor when he declared war on the United States. Churchill breathed a double sigh of relief.

It is useful to reflect on history, on the details of history, for they reveal the highly contingent nature of world events. The study of history can also stimulate our thinking about current events and generate powerful insights.

The Lend-Lease program provided Britain with the oxygen it needed to continue its armed resistance against Nazi aggression. Without it, Britain could have fallen, and without Britain it could have taken the Allies decades to defeat Germany.

Military aid to Ukraine is similar in many ways to the Lend-Lease assistance to Great Britain. Without the latter, Britain could have fallen. Without the former, Ukraine could suffer defeat at the hands of the Russians1 Or the situation could deteriorate to such a degree that NATO combat forces become directly involved.

Pearl Harbor happened 82 years ago, but it remains a vivid reminder of the fact that American isolationism, whatever its short-term benefits including financial savings, may turn out to be extremely costly in the end.

Today, in South America Venezuela is threatening to invade and annex part of Guyana. This is but a small harbinger of what might occur around the globe if Ukraine falls, and with it the fundamental pillars of international law and the U.N. Charter-based international legal order.

The 82nd anniversary of Pearl Harbor is a good day to reflect on the big picture, and what is really involved in resisting Russian aggression in Ukraine.

FURTHER READING

1) George Packer, "'We Only Need Some Metal Things'; Will America abandon Ukraine?" The Atlantic, December 9, 2023 (7:32 am ET).[78]

2) James Rowles,"As the Global South turns away from the West, the West should curtail its financial support and trade preferences for the Global South," The Trenchant Observer, September 27, 2023.[79]

3) James Rowles, "Ukraine War, September 27, 2023: Experts agree--The international order is crumbling," The Trenchant Observer, September 27, 2023.[80]

Part Five

Trump and the Supreme Court: Disqualification

22

January 4, 2024

Trump and Section 3
of the 14th Amendment

David French, in an op-ed column in the *New York Times* on January 4, 2024, lays out in cogent arguments why the Supreme Court should apply the plain text of the Constitution and hold that Donald Trump is barred from running for president by Section 3 of the 14th Amendment.[81]

Section 3 of the 14th Amendment[82] to the U.S. Constitution provides the following:

Fourteenth Amendment Equal Protection and Other Rights
Section 3 Disqualification from Holding Office
No person shall be a Senator or Representative in Congress, or elector of President and Vice-President, or hold any office, civil or military, under the United States, or under any State, who, having previously taken an oath, as a member of Congress, or as an officer of the United States, or as a member of any State legislature, or as an executive or judicial officer of any State, to support the Constitution of the United States, shall have engaged in insurrection or rebellion against the same, or given aid or comfort to the enemies thereof. But Congress may by a vote of two-thirds of each House, remove such disability.

Part of the breakdown in the Rule of Law in the United States is revealed by the number of calls for the Supreme Court to decide the case of Trump's disqualification to run for president, one way or another, on the basis of political and/or practical arguments.

This reflects the widespread view, not without justification, that the Supreme Court acts on the basis of political considerations in important cases.

The prime example is its decision in *Bush v. Gore* in 2000 in which it decided the presidential election in favor of George W. Bush.

The Court reversed the decision of the Florida Supreme Court which had ordered a recount which would have given victory to Gore in Florida and with it the electoral votes to become president.

Since the Florida Court's decision was based in part on Florida law, the Supreme Court could not reverse the decision without basing its decision on a provision in the U.S. Constitution and a Constitutional right based on such a provision.

No such right existed under the Court's previous rulings.

So the Supreme Court pulled a rabbit out of the hat, and by tortured reasoning found the Florida Court's decision violated the equal protection clause of the 14th Amendment. Moreover, the Court held that its decision, which was based on no precedent, could not be cited as a precedent for the new right it had created out of thin air.

In this manner, the Supreme Court decided the future course of American history.

Think of it: Bush's invasion of Afghanistan after September 11, 2001, Bush's invasion of Iraq in 2003, Bush's use of torture in secret CIA prisons and at Abu Gharib, and much more.

It is not an overstatement to say that the Supreme Court's decision in *Bush v. Gore* changed the direction of U.S. history, and not in a good way.

The decision cost the Supreme Court much of its legitimacy and authority in the coming years, as the process of nomination and confirmation of Supreme Court justices became overtly political.

Senate Majority Leader Mitch McConnell refused to allow hearings or a floor vote on Barack Obama's nomination of Merrick Garland in 2016, depriving the Democrats of a justice they had nominated who surely would have been confirmed had McConnell not resorted to strong-arm tactics in the Senate to thwart such an outcome.

After Donald Trump became President in 2017, he nominated Neil Gorsuch to the Court. Gorsuch was confirmed in a bitterly-contested partisan vote in the Republican-controlled Senate.

Let us now hope that the Supreme Court will uphold the Rule of Law by applying the plain text of Section 3 of the 14th Amendment and ruling that Donald Trump is disqualified from running for president in 2024–or ever again.2

It is time to end the politicization of the Supreme Court. Pulling another rabbit out the hat to ignore Section 3 would destroy what is left of the Court's legitimacy and authority.

In contrast, a decision based on the plain text of Section 3 of the 14th Amendment would be a necessary and important step toward restoring the authority of the Court.

Should the Court nonetheless ignore the plain language of Section 3, Congress should expand the composition of the Court in order to dilute its partisan political role.

UPDATE:

See Gerard N. Magliocca, "What the Supreme Court Should Not Do in Trump's Disqualification Case, New York Times, January 5, 2024.[83]

Comment by Michael Mauldin[84]

It seems simple. I believe Trump to be guilty of treason. But unfortunately he has not had his day in court.

Reply by James Rowles (Author)[85]

Thanks for your comment, Michael.

Section 3 of the 14th amendment applies to those eho "shall have engaged in insurrection or rebellion against the (U.S.) or given aid or comfort to the enemies thereof." Shibboleths like "everyone has a right to his day in court" depend on context to be true. Slaveholders did not have a right to a day in court before slaves became free under the 13th Amendment.

Nonetheless, in fact in the Colorado judicial proceedings Trump did have his day in court. And he will in Maine as well, though he already did have a chance to participate in an administrative proceeding prior to the Secretary of State's ruling that he was ineligible to be on the ballot.

It's a simple matter of applying the plain language of the Constitution. In banana republics, there are endless arguments about why the plain text of the law should not be applied. Are we becoming a banana republic?

Courts and judges must be courageous and overcome any fear they may have of the violent reactions of Trump's supporters. They and their families must be provided with all necessary security to ensure their personal safety and that of their staffs.

Sometimes the rule of law comes down to black and white, not the endless speculations of commentators on the cable news programs.

It may come down to "Gunfight at the OK Corral".

Abraham Lincoln faced that and upheld the Constitution.

Do we and the Supreme Court have the courage to do the same?

23

January 31, 2024

Donald Trump Seems to be a Mega-Criminal

The Presumption of Innocence Does Not Apply to Political Judgments. Moreover, Section 3 of the 14th Amendment Applies Not Just to Trump, but also to His Many Accomplices.

The presumption of innocence in the case of Donald Trump applies only to his trials and eventual criminal convictions. It does not apply to political judgments about his actions.

There is a common misconception that it is improper to speak of an individual as having committed a crime unless and until he is convicted of a criminal offense in a court proceeding. The "presumption of innocence", however, applies only to the trial and criminal conviction of a defendant charged with committing a crime. It does not apply to making political or moral judgments, outside of this judicial context, about an individual's actions. This fact is particularly relevant when there is abundant evidence in the public record of the individual having committed the crime.

One reason people shy away from calling a crime a crime and a criminal a criminal is their fear of being sued for libel and defamation.

Newspapers and others use the formulaic term of "alleged crime(s)" in order to protect themselves from the costs and distractions of defending themselves against lawsuits for libel and defamation. Legally, absent actual malice (knowingly making a false statement), they have the right to speak of "crimes", pure and simple, in the case of a public figure such as Trump. This is constitutionally-protected free speech under the 1964 Supreme Court case of *New York Times v. Sullivan.* Individuals can similarly avoid the inconvenience of litigation by using the "alleged crime" formula.

These legal issues, however, should not prevent us from forming political judgments about crimes and those who have apparently committed them.

Consequently, we don't need a court of law to declare Donald Trump guilty of the many crimes he appears to have committed,[86] often in broad daylight, in order for us to be able to speak of his apparent crimes.[87] His guilt appears tobe amply confirmed by the evidence in the public record, including that referred to in the 91 criminal indictments against him.[88]

We are speaking about making political judgments here, not about his formal criminal conviction in a court of law.

Trump seems to be the political equivalent to a mafia boss, using bevies of lawyers to delay all proceedings against him until after the November 5, 2024 election. If he wins, he is likely to discontinue all federal criminal proceedings against him and his accomplices. He has said that he would pardon many of those who have been convicted of criminal offenses related to the January 6, 2021 insurrection and invasion of the Capitol

Trump appears to be a mega-criminal. The public and the voting electorate should feel free to consider Trump guilty, as a matter of political opinion, in all cases where the public evidence is strong. He is apparently a mega-felon, and if justice is allowed to run its course, he is extremely likely to be convicted of the crimes for which he has been charged.

The American electorate should not be misled to believe that they may not consider Trump to be a criminal until he is formally convicted of criminal offenses in a court of law. The American people, and our political system, are not that stupid.

Moreover, Trump should not even be allowed to run for the presidency, given the express wording of Section 3 of the 14th Amendment to the Constitution, which provides:

Fourteenth Amendment Equal Protection and Other Rights Section 3 Disqualification from Holding Office

No person shall be a Senator or Representative in Congress, or elector of President and Vice-President, or hold any office, civil or military, under the United States, or under any State, who, having previously taken an oath, as a member of Congress, or as an officer of the United States, or as a member of any State legislature, or as an executive or judicial officer of any State, to support the Constitution of the United States, shall have engaged in insurrection or rebellion against the same, or given aid or comfort to the enemies thereof. But Congress may by a vote of two-thirds of each House, remove such disability.[89]

If, despite the plain wording of Section 3, the Supreme Court allows Trump to run in the November presidential election, and if he wins, we will have elected an apparent mafia-style crime boss and his henchmen to run the United States.

A further word regarding Section 3 of the 14th Amendment is in order.

Section 3 would appear to apply not only to Trump, but also to all of the Senators and House Members and other federal and state officials who, having taken an oath to uphold the Constitution of the United States), "have engaged in insurrection or rebellion against the same, or given aid or comfort to the enemies thereof."

Consequently, all such officials should be barred from running for public office under Section 3 of the 14th Amendment.

If citizens are paying attention, a large number of lawsuits should be initiated to prevent such persons from running for public office.

The issue here is whether the citizens of a democracy such as the United States will act forcefully to defend that democracy against those who would overthrow both the Constitution and the Rule of Law.

24

February 7, 2024

Disqualification of Senate and House Candidates Under the 14th Amendment

S houldn't the Constitution's "Disqualification Clause—Section 3 of the 14th Amendment—apply not only to Donald Trump, but also to Josh Hawley, Ted Cruz, and other Senate and House candidates who opposed the certification of the 2020 election results?[90]

The following Senators and House Representatives are among those who voted against the certification of the presidential election results on January 6, 2021.

Senators
> Josh Hawley (R-MO)
> Ted Cruz (R-TX)
> Tommy Tuberville (R-AL)

Representatives
> Mike Rogers (R-AL)
> Darrell Issa (R-CA)
> Devin Nunes (R-CA)

Lauren Boebert (R-CO)
Matt Gaetz (R-FL)
Marjorie Greene (R-GA)
Steve Scalise (R-LA)
David Cawthorn (R-NC)
Jim Jordan (R-OH)
Elise Stefanik (R-NY)

A number of these individuals, including Josh Hawley and Ted Cruz, are running for reelection in 2024.[91]

A strong case can be made that those who voted against certification were part of a conspiracy to overthrow the November 2020 presidential election results, and with them the Constitution. They appear to have "engaged in insurrection or rebellion against the (U.S.), or given aid or comfort to the enemies thereof," in the words of Section 31

Section 3 of the 14th Amendment[92] to the U.S. Constitution provides the following:

Fourteenth Amendment Equal Protection and Other Rights
Section 3 Disqualification from Holding Office

> No person shall be a Senator or Representative in Congress, or elector of President and Vice-President, or hold any office, civil or military, under the United States, or under any State, who, having previously taken an oath, as a member of Congress, or as an officer of the United States, or as a member of any State legislature, or as an executive or judicial officer of any State, to support the Constitution of the United States, shall have engaged in insurrection or rebellion against the same, or given aid or comfort to the enemies the same.

Consequently, those who voted against certification, including those listed above, would appear to be prime candidates for disqualification from running for reelection in 2024.

If citizens are paying attention, a large number of lawsuits should be initiated to prevent such persons from running for public office.

The issue here is whether the citizens of a democracy such as the United States will act to defend that democracy against those who would overthrow the Constitution and the Rule of Law.

To this observer, it seems that the Republicans are on a total war footing, and are willing to follow Donald Trump to the ends of the earth, and to the end of our Constitution.

Following Donald Trump, the great admirer of Vladimir Putin, Republicans in Congress have succeeded to date in blocking passage of urgently-needed military and economic assistance for Ukraine. Putin couldn't be happier.

The likely Republican presidential candidate is a pro-Russian supporter of the monstrous dictator and war criminal Vladimir Putin, president of the Russian Federation.

A battle for the soul and the future of the country is underway.

And yet the Democrats seem to be asleep, and incapable of acting together forcefully to avoid what is a looming catastrophe, not only for the United States but also for Ukraine, international law, and the U.N. Charter-based international legal order.

Those opposing Trump and his fascist movement are in an existential struggle to uphold and strengthen tbe Rule of Law, both under the U.S. Constitution and the United Nations Charter.

If Democrats and "little d" democrats are to prevail in this struggle, they need to pull out all the stops and shift to a war footing.

One of the first things they should do is to put together a billion-dollar legal defense fund to finance an all-out effort to disqualify those who supported the insurrection and attempt to overthrow the Constitution, or who aided those who did, from running for election to the House or the Senate in 2024.

Successfully executing such a strategy could return a comfortable working majority for the Democrats in the House, and potentially help them achieve a majority in the Senate.

Moreover, a major benefit would be to remove from the Congress the despicable legislators who betrayed our country and the Constitution on January 6, and on the days leading up to that culmination of criminal efforts to overthrow the 2020 election.

As the French shouted in the days of the French Revolution, "Aux armes, Citoyens!!! (Get your weapons, Citizens!) In 2024, under the Rule of Law and the Constitution, those weapons are lawsuits to prevent the despicable individuals who tried to overthrow the Constitution from ever running for public office again.

As mandated by Section 3 of the 14th Amendment of the United States Constitution.

25

March 16, 2024

Trump v. Anderson.
Rogue Supreme Court.
What Can be Done?

Expand the Court. We are not entirely
helpless, despite how it feels

The U.S. Supreme Court has decided, in *Trump v. Anderson*, for all intents and purposes, to write Section 3 of the 14th Amendment out of the Constitution.[93]

In *Bush v. Gore (2000)*, the Court interfered even more egregiously in a presidential contest, in effect awarding the presidency to George W. Bush.

Now it is making decisions that allow Donald Trump to delay his trials.[94] It's decision to overturn the Colorado Supreme Court's decision barring Trump from the ballot was a lame decision. It was a dishonorable decision. It was a decision viewed by many as that of a corrupt Supreme Court. That of a rogue Supreme Court.

Or, as George Conway suggests in his article in *The Atlantic*, that of a *fearful* Supreme Court.[95]

Particularly significant is the opinion of J. Michael Luttig and Laurence H. Tribe, preeminent Constitutional law experts—conservative

101

and liberal, respectively—in which they concur in the views expressed by Conway and in this column, though they take no position on the issue of expansion of the membership of the Court.[96]

Particularly disappointing was the fact that. the liberal justices of the Court went along with the decision.

The decision may have been based on fear on the part of one or more of the justices. None would want to be, together with their families, targets for MAGA zealots. Violence is in the air. The possibility of fascist violence against the justices or their family members is palpable and cannot be ruled out.

One may recall reports that some Republican votes in the impeachment trials of Donald Trump were influenced by fears of physical violence.

Colorado erred by not choosing a preeminent Supreme Court advocate to argue its case before the Supreme Court. Such an advocate might have been able to prevent the Court from lurching toward the exit ramp on the specious ground that different state supreme courts might reach different decisions, and one of them might be able to decide who would be the next president of the United States.

But as Convay points out, the Court wanted to reverse the Colotado Supreme Court decision, and the Constitution and the law had little to do with their decision.

Had it wanted to uphold the Colorado *Anderson* decision, the Court could have easily set forth uniform standards for the application of Section 3 of the 14th Amendment by state courts, as it had repeatedly done in abortion cases prior to overthrowing *Roe v. Wade.*

The sad truth is that there were no justices with sufficient courage to take a full-throated position in defense of applying Section 3 as its drafters intended, and as those who voted in state legislatures to ratify the 14th Amendment intended.

It is instructive to take a look at other countries.

Brazil's Electoral Court has barred former President Jair Bolsonaro from running for office before 2030 because of his commission of electoral crimes.[97] This decision is without prejudice to further legal penalties to be assessed against Bolsonaro for other crimes, including leading an insurrection on January 8, 2023.

Which country is the Banana Republic, Brazil or the United States?

The remedy for a rogue Supreme Court like the one we have now in the U.S. is fairly obvious: We must expand the membership of the Court, to either 12 or 15 justices.

Expansion to 15 members could be done in stages.

In the corresponding Supreme Court reform bill, care should be taken to eliminate the role of partisan politics in the selection and confirmation of new justices. A vote of two-thirds or at least 60% of the Senate should be required for confirmation, with no exceptions, and a mechanism to guarantee that a floor vote on any nominee will be held in a timely manner should be enacted.

Supreme Court reform is no longer a matter of purely theoretical concern.

It is now a vital element in efforts to save our democracy.

FURTHER READING

Drew Goins, "It takes a lot to get a federal judge to write a piece this bold," WashingtonPost, October 7, 2024 (4:52 p.m. EDT).[98]

26

February 15, 2024

Putin Says He Prefers Biden over Trump in Presidential Election

How will Trump react?

Vladimir Putin has said at a press conference that he prefers Joe Biden over Donald Trump in the American presidential election in November, 2024.[99] Der Spiegel reports:[100]

(O)n the evening of Valentine's Day, Vladimir Putin surprised many with astonishingly clear words in support of Democrat Biden. When asked by a Russian journalist what outcome he hopes for from the American presidential election, Putin said: "Biden, he is more experienced. He is predictable, he is an old-school politician." In addition, Putin defended the Democrat against (malicious comments) because of his old age. "When I met Mr. Biden three years ago, people actually already talked about his shortcomings, but I didn't see anything like that," Putin said.

Russia experts think he is serious.

On the other hand, the old KGB master could be trying to defuse Democratic criticisms against Trump for being a stalking horse for Putin who would end U.S. support for Ukraine and weaken NATO.

It seems like Putin is serious. Whatever the truth, it will be interesting to see how Trump reacts, not just immediately but over time.

Whatever the logic, even if Putin's statement is a ploy to help Trump, given his nature Trump will find it hard not to react to what seems to be a betrayal by his buddy Putin.

If and when he does react, his reaction could release the Republicans in the House and those remaining Senators who oppose aid for Ukraine from any mandate from Trump to oppose such aid.

If and when that happens, the aid-for-Ukraine bill, which already passed the Senate, should sail through the House and quickly become law.

FURTHER READING

1) James Rowles, "In a country with no memory, Donald Trump and his fascist Republican Party may win in November," Trenchant Observations, February 9, 2024.[101]

2) James Rowles, "Disqualification of Senators Josh Hawley, Ted Cruz, and other Senate and House candidates under Section 3 of the 14th Amendment; Comment on the Day's News: Putin is watching Biden's actions in Gaza," Trenchant Observations, February 7, 2024.[102]

3) James Rowles, "REPRISE: A moment for reflection: The 85th anniversary of Kristallnacht, November 9-10, 1938; Plus: A selection of some of the best articles for current and new readers," Trenchant Observations, February 2, 2024.[103]

Part Six

Europe Changed. The World Changed. The Long Road of War that Lies Before Us

27

March 18, 2024

Europe and the World Changed. The Long Road of War That Lies Before Us

Remembering Stefan Zweig and his book
The World of Yesterday (1942)

The Author has translated this article from the original Spanish text of an article published here,[104] *without any use of artificial intelligence. Slight revisions to the English text have been made.*

In 1900, Europe and America enjoyed a peace which, except for the Civil War (1861-1865) and the wars against the Indians, had lasted more than 80 years, that is, roughly the same time that passed between 1945 and 2024.

The phenomenon of war had been overcome, people believed, except for a few armed conflicts limited in time and space such as the Crimean War (1853-1856), the War between Prussia and Austria-Hungary (1866), and War between Prussia and France (1870-1871).

To be sure, there were crises, and a naval arms race, but for the great majority of the population in Europe, war seemed almost inconceivable.

The situation was somewhat like that in Europe and America today, except of course for the war in Ukraine. The Korean War (1950-1953) and the Vietnam War (1964-1975) were major wars which, however, did not threaten the homeland. Moreover, they happened a long time ago.

The Gulf War (1990-1991), the War in Afghanistan (2001-2021), and the Iraq War (2003-2017) were wars of a different kind. None of these wars was an existential conflict in which there was a real possibility of defeat either for the United Stats or for Europe.

War in the sense of World War I and World War II, in which the future of the Western countries was at stake, was virtually unknown between 1945 and 2022, when Russia launched a full-scale invasion of Ukraine. War, in the sense of the destruction of cities and the deaths of hundreds of thousands or millions of people, *of our people*, was unknown, while memories of World War II had largely faded.

The Russian aggression against Ukraine in 2022, accompanied by war crimes and crimes against humanity on a massive scale, gave rise to deep apprehension among the population in Europe, but the European governments (and the U.S.) declared to their peoples their firm commitment to not let themselves get involved in a war with Russia.

Notwithstanding the fact that the energy crisis caused by the Russian sanctions hit many Europeans very hard,[105] the populations in Europe, except in the Baltics and in Central and Eastern Europe, had confidence in the declarations of their governments that there would be no threat of war with Russia. It would be sufficient to support Ukraine with military and economic assistance "as long as it takes".

Or at least so it appeared.

Until French President Emmanuel Macron declared at a summit of defense ministers in Paris on February 26 that European and NATO countries should not exclude the possibility of sending troops to Ukraine.[106]

His commentary gave rise to a storm of criticism for having suggested that the war could come to touch leaders and their countrymen personally.

Suddenly, the leaders and their populations were forced to think not only of Ukraine's war of self-defense, but also of their own self-defense in a potential war launched by Russia against them.

Together with doubts and delays regarding the promised $60 billion dollars of American military aid for Ukraine, blocked by Republicans in the House acting on the instructions of Donald Trump, and the realistic possibility that Trump might return to the White House in January 2025, the war seemed closer and closer, and even to be "Our War", as Nicolas Tenzer argued forcefully in his new book, *Nôtre Guerre (2024)*.[107]

Slowly, Europeans began to understand that the road to peace is going to be very long, and that it might pass through long stretches of war.

Although Russia invaded Ukraine in 2014, and Georgia earlier in 2008, only now are Europeans beginning to understand that War has returned to Europe, and that it is going to accompany each of them for decades if not for the rest of their lives.

Europe changed, in a profound sense. The world changed.[108]

As in 1914.

As in 1939.

And it will never again be the same as it was.

28

March 22, 2024

Ukraine: The Frozen Strategy of Joe Biden and the West

and its Portents for an Endless War, or Possible Defeat

T he war in Ukraine is already a "frozen conflict". But what is frozen is not only the trench warfare on the front lines, but also the strategic thinking in the White House and some NATO capitals, such as Berlin.

While the Europeans are beginning to grasp what is at stake in the war, and to grapple with the possibility of a Trump presidency, the strategic thinking in the White House is frozen, controlled by an aging man frightened by Vladimir Putin's threats of nuclear war.

Joe Biden is critizized because of his age. But the gaffes and memory glitches on television are not the core of the problem. The core of the problem is that Biden evidences the rigid thinking and inflexibility that is often though not always characteristic of men of advancing age.

Added to that is the fact that Biden was never known for the acuity of his foreign policy judgment. As former Secretary of Defense Bob Gates observed in his 2014 memoir, "I think he has been wrong on nearly every major foreign policy and national security issue over the past four decades."[109]

Moreover, Biden has failed to put together a strong foreign policy team.

His principal advisers are his former srtaffers, Jake Sullivan and Antony Blinken. His Defense Secretary, Lloyd Austin, is a member of a small coterie of national security officials and former officials who have joined together in a private consulting firm.

Austin appears to have been chosen on the basis of identity politics. While he has done an able job in executing Biden's foreign policy, he has not shown brilliance or creativity in shaping foreign policy. There is a reason the law provides that military leaders must have left the service for seven years before they can be appointed to be Defense Secretary. Biden's grant of a waiver in Austin's case ignored the rationale behind that provision.

The one thing that is common to Biden's foreign policy advisers is that they are not likely to challenge his positions.

The one person who might have demonstrated independence of judgment, Susan Rice, the former U.N. Ambassador and Assistant Secrtary of State for Africa, was shunted off to head the White House Domestic Policy Council. She resigned in 2023.

Jake Sullivan, the National Security Adviser, appears to have eclipsed Secretary of State Antony Blinken and others on Biden's foreign policy team. Biden once referred to Sullivan as a "once-in-a-generation" brilliant mind.

He has Biden's solid support, and with it has risen to be Biden's principal foreign policy adviser.

Sullivan *is* brilliant, in an academic and analytical and information-processing sense. But he has never served overseas in a foreign policy role, and indeed seems to have had very little experience on the ground overseas. He lacks the kind of on-the- ground experience that a former ambassador has, and yet is sent by Biden to talk to foreign leaders instead of the Secretary of State.

Biden's rigidity of thinking was dramatically demonstrated by his ill-considered decision in April 2021 to withdraw **all** Americans from Afghanistan, overruling his military advisers and then lying about the fact.

By withdrawing all contractors as well as soldiers, Biden guaranteed that the Afghan Air Force could not fly, and that without the Air Force the Afghan Army could not fight. This made the fall of the regime of Ashraf Ghani, the democratically-elected President of Afghanistan, inevitable.

Biden's and his administration's criticisms of Ghani and the Afghan Army for being unwilling to fight were utterly shameful.

On Ukraine, Biden's statement that NATO forces would not intervene in Ukraine if Russia invaded that country greatly undercut the deterrent force of NATO and U.S. forces.

Before and at the time of the invasion on February 24, 2024, Biden and the EU were very slow to threaten or actually impose the most serious sanctions on Russia. One can never know, but perhaps as a result, at least in part, deterrence failed.

Since the invasion, Biden has manifested extraordinary rigidity in his strategic thinking about the conduct of the war.

First, he has consistently refused and/or delayed the transfer of modern weapons systems to Ukraine, or blocked their transfer by others, from the introduction of the HIMARS artillery units to the transfer of Abrams tanks and F16 fighter aircraft.

Second, Biden has enforced a rule that no weapons transferred by the U.S. or other NATO countries may be used by Ukraine to attack targets in Russia proper or the Kerch Strait Bridge. He has thus prevented Ukraine from using these weapons as they have every right to do in exercise of the right of self-defense under international law and Article 51 of the United Nations Charter. He has, in effect, forced Ukraine to fight with one hand tied behind its back, unable to strike bases in Russia from which missiles and drones are launched against its cities and civilian infrastructure, such as the electrical system, dams, and other civilian targets including schools, hospitals, churches and other institutions protected by International Humanitarian Law.

Third, Biden, NATO, the EU, and other nations supporting Ukraine have failed to ramp up their production of weapons sand weapons systems and in particular artillery shells and other munitions to meet Ukraine's military requirements. Moreover, it is shocking to learn that European countries are only now considering prohibitions on exports of munitions to third countries, where much of their production has been going—sold for a nice profit.

In the face of a likely drawn-out war, the U.S. and the West have failed to move to a wartime economy that might guarantee production of the weapons and other munitions that it was foreseeable would be needed by Ukraine in such a conflict.

Fourth, failing to take the constraints of peremptory norms of international law (*jus cogens*) into account, the U.S. and major Western allies of Ukraine proceeded on the assumption that a peace settlement (or ceasefire "freezng" the conflict) with Vladimir Putin and Russia was possible.

Such a settlement would have required what were euphemistically called "territorial concessions"—i.e., cession to Russia of territories it had conquered by aggression and the illegal use of military force.

Such "territorial concessions", moreover, would have involved the surrender of millions of Ukrainian citizens to occupying Russian troops which have routinely engaged in assassinations, torture, the abduction and removal to Russia of thousands of Ukrainian children, and the subjection of the population to a military force of almost unimaginable brutality.

The Russians have been guilty of an ongoing pattern of war crimes on a massive scale, crimes against humanity, and in the last analysis acts of genocide, committed by definition with genocidal intent. Russia represents absolute Evil. Its military strategy has been based on the intentional use of terror .

Fifth, Biden and the U.S. have failed to energetically press the countries of the so-called "Global South", the fence-sitters, to join the sanctions regimes adopted by the U.S., the EU and other countries against Russia, with the goal of bringing that country's economy down and support for the war to a halt. This generally *laissez-faire* approach to the imposition of sanctions by countries in the so-called Global South has been a major factor in the failure of the sanctions to achieve their intended objectives.

The overarching failure of the Biden administration has been its failure to understand the big picture and the stakes in Russia's war of aggression against Ukraine, and to relate specific decisions to that larger understanding.

To be sure, there have been some successes.

After telegraphing to Putin that the U.S. and NATO would not intervene militarily if Russia invaded Ukraine, and having failed to deter the invasion, the U.S. and its NATO allies and the EU did succeed in maintaining unity in their responses to Russia's aggression and war crimes.

Unfortunately, this unity—particularly in the first year or two—seemed to be built on agreement on the least demanding position among NATO members.

The basic consensus was formed around two propositions. First, NATO countries would provide military and economic assistance to Ukraine sufficient to avoid defeat at the hands of the Russians. Second, NATO countries would not become directly involved militarily in the conflict.

The ultimate question—was the goal merely to avoid defeat, or also to secure victory over Russia?—was basically glossed over with the disingenuous formulation that NATO and EU countries would support Ukraine "for as long as it takes".

As long as it takes for what? To avoid defeat? To achieve victory? The answer was fudged in a way that allowed both camps to repeat the mantra.

A singular achievement of the NATO countries has been the expansion of NATO to include Finland and Sweden. The Biden administration deserves great credit for helping to overcome Turkish objections to Sweden's entry into the alliance.

A related success has been the progressive stiffening of EU sanctions against Russia. The members of the EU deserve the greatest credit for this achievement. However, the Biden administration also deserves considerable credit for its success in coordinating Russian sanctions with the EU.

Nonetheless, there have been significant and glaring failures, in addition to those outlined above.

One glaring failure has been the failure to secure the expulsion of Russia from the G-20. The very fact that officials from Western democracies continue to meet with Russian officials within the framework of the G-20 is scandalous and shameful beyond any words of description.

Putin is guilty of the international crime of aggression, while Russia is currently engaged in the systematic commission of war crimes, crimes against humanity and the crime of genocide against the Ukrainian people.

Russia continues a frontal assault on international law and the U.N. Charter-based international legal order, and indeed on our entire modern civilization based on reason and law.

It is deeply shameful and a betrayal of our deepest values for representatives of the United States and other Western democracies to sit down with representatives of a regime which represents the embodiment of pure evil. The U.S. and other democracies should push vigorously for the expulsion of Russia from the G-20.

If they are unable to achieve this, they should simply withdraw from the G-20. They should absolutely shun Russia and its representatives, everywhere.

A second major failure has been the failure of Joe Biden and the Biden administration to successfully convince he American people that the outcome of the war in Ukraine is of paramount importance, that it will demand great sacrifices from the American people, and that it will determine the nature of the world their children will inherit.

Conclusion

It is not so much Biden's frailty and increasing memory lapses that are so threatening, as it is the rigidity in his thinking, and the fact that he never had particularly good foreign policy judgment to begin with.

The rigidity in Biden's thinking is extraordinarily consequential in terms of U.S. strategy in foreign policy in general, and in the struggle with Russia in particular.

This rigidity is all the more concerning in view of his very stubborn and prideful character.

Biden has done a great job as a domestic president, on the whole.

Compared to Donald Trump, a cunning and dangerous fascist, Biden is a paragon of reason and wise decision making. Yet fear of Trump should not deter Biden's closest allies from insisting that he make changes in the area of foreign policy, for the good of the country.

U.S. strategy in Ukraine is not likely to change, or to change quickly enough to avoid a long, drawn-out war, or defeat, so long as Biden is president, and so long as he does not replace his current foreign policy team, or at least strengthen it with outside advisers of great stature.

Part Seven

Biden Versus Trump

29

May 7, 2024

In a Country with no Memory, Donald Trump May Win

Originally published on February 9, 2024

At no point before 1933 did the outlook for Adolf Hitler and the fascists in Germany look as favorable as it does now for Donald Trump and the fascists in the United States.

In America , a country with no memory, Donald Trump and his fascist1 Republican Party may win in November.

Political leaders and journalists speak of Donald Trump now as if he's just another candidate.

They assume the population and likely voters remember why there are 91 criminal indictments against Trump, that he has been found guilty of sexual battery amounting to rape in a civil trial (where in a civil trial rape was not charged), that over 60 courts all rejected Republican charges that there was fraud in the 2020 presidential election, that Donald Trump insti-gated an insurrection that included the invasion of the Capitol causing five deaths and many injuries to policemen–as Trump passively watched on TV, and that he was also the mastermind of a well-orchestrated attempt, both before and on January 6, to overthrow the November 2020 election results.

They may even assume, if they remember themselves, that the population remembers the ten felony cases of obstruction of justice Robert Mueller laid out in great detail in his Report on April 18, 2019.

But if they are making such assumptions, they are dead wrong.

America has become a country with no memory.

Neil Postman in his classic study, *Amusing Ourselves to Death (1985)*, qotes Bill Moyers' insightful observation, as follows:

We Americans seem to know everything about the last twenty-four hours but very little of the last sixty centuries or the last sixty years.2

Postman describes the shift from the "Typographic world" based on the printing press and the written word, to the current world shaped by the television commercial, which he terms "the Age of Show Business and Image Politics". His analysis is deep, and goes far in helping the reader to understand the appeal of Donald Trump, the Entertainer, as opposed to that of Joe Biden, the Politician.

In such a memory void, where truth and actual facts have no weight, or at best a diminishing influence that vanishes after weeks, or even months, a charlatan and accused felon like Donald Trump can appear on television and weave his web of lies and distortions almost without commentary.

We are not living in a rational world, where truth and remembered facts may influence the opinions of voters and the votes they actually cast.

As a fascist takeover "with American characteristics" draws nearer, we must in all candor report on the failures of the many political leaders in both parties which have accelerated the growth of fascism in the United States.

First of all, there are the many Republican leaders who have either surrendered to their fear of Trump and his supporters, have abandoned all principles and their oaths to uphold the Constitution in blind pursuit of personal ambition, or who have succumbed to ideology and beliefs that Trump will be better for the country—and for their companies' earnings and their own pocketbooks—due to cuts in taxes and other decisions supposedly favoring business.

Fear, ambition, and ideology (often at variance with the facts) have all contributed to the growth of the Cult of Trump and of fascism in the United States.

Would-be authoritarians and fascists will always exist. But what has contributed to the extraordinary growth in their numbers in the U.S. in recent years has been not only the failures of the Republicans but also the failures of the Democrats and Independents and other small-d "democratic" opponents of Trump, to take resolute action to stop Trump and his fascist supporters.

Foremost among the failures on the Democratic side have been those of President Joe Biden and Attorney General Merrick Garland, who for some two years refused to initiate criminal proceedings against Trump and his accomplices for the apparent blatant commission of multiple felonies. These crimes ranged from cases of Obstruction of Justice (e.g., as outlined in the Mueller Report) to the numerous apparent crimes committed in Trump's many efforts to overthrow the results of the November 3, 2020 election.

For a very long time House Democratic Leader Nancy Pelosi blocked all efforts by Democratic members of the House to launch a full and broad investigation into Trump's alleged crimes. Finally, after almost two years, in September 2019 she allowed the Democrats to carry out a narrow impeachment investigation of Trump. In December, 2019 the House impeached Trump on two counts related to pressuring Ukrainian President Volodymyr Zelenski to provide information against Hunter Biden for Trump's personal political purposes. While the proof was overwhelming, enough Republicans violated their oaths of office to prevent Trump's conviction and removal in his Senate trial.

After the January 6, 2021 Insurrection, Pelosi allowed the House Democrats to impeach Trump a second time. Republican Senate Leader Mitch McConnell delayed the Senate impeachment trial until after Trump left office, and then with other Republicans voted against finding Trump guilty of the impeachment charges on the ground that he was no longer in office.

Again, though also by a narrower margin, Republicans violating their oaths of office blocked Trump's conviction.

At the Justice Department, Merrick Garland, after swearing in his confirmation hearings he would not let political considerations influence his decisions, did precisely that by not immediately launching broad investigations into Trump's apparent crimes.

Finally, on November 18, 2022, Garland appointed Jack Smith as a Special Prosecutor to investigate Trump's potential crimes. So far Smith has succeeded in obtaining multiple criminal indictments against Trump, both for his attempt to overthrow the election, and for his violation of secrecy laws regarding highly sensitive intelligence information, including information regarding nuclear secrets.

Nonetheless, Garland allowed the statute of limitations to run out on the 10 Obstruction of Justice cases detailed, with references to specific evidence, in Robert Mueller's Report of April 18, 2019.

The alleged crimes were committed in the spring of 2017.

Garland allowed the five-year statute of limitations on these major felonies to expire in 2022, without comment.

Instead of applying the law, Garland was apparently attuned to the political realities, and the fact that America has no memory.

The final shortcoming of the Democrats has been their failure to develop a viable alternative to Biden, a younger candidate who, without Biden's age and foreign policy leadership liabilities (e.g., the decision to withdraw from Afghanistan), might help the Democrats run a strong and winning campaign against Trump and his supporters.

Given Biden's adamant refusal to step aside, they have failed further by not developing and demanding the naming of a strong vice-presidential candidate who, unlike Kamala Harris, might be viewed as someone who is ready and prepared to become a capable president.

Identity politics may have made such a move appear to be impossible in the eyes of Democratic leaders. Nonetheless, such a move might represent the best possibility for a Democratic victory in 2024. Sometimes in exceptional situations political leaders need to reach beyond conventional wisdom to find and implement bold solutions that might save the day.

The choice is stark: Stick with your identity politics and probably lose, or replace Harris with someone who is viewed as good potential president, and win the election.

The latter option would in all likelihood remove, or at least greatly diminish, the issue of Biden's age as a factor in the election.

Instead of pushing for such dramatic action, Democrats, with folded hands, have been passively observing Biden as he drags tho party down to what may be a resounding defeat.

They should take the polls seriously, which show that Trump has moved from a dead heat with Biden to a widening lead—as high as five or six points in some recent national polls. Moreover, these are national polls. The situation may be worse in the swing states whose electoral votes may decide the election, such as Michigan.

Democrats don't get the central point: A majority of voters just don't like Biden. This is not fair. This is not rational. But it is a fact.

In a world ruled by mass political emotions impervious to facts, Biden is losing support. The polls tell a clear and increasingly devastating tale of Biden's looming defeat. He is likely to take a lot of Democrats down with him.

Despite his many merits, Biden is a weak candidate. Vice President Kamala Harris was a poor choice for VP in 2020, and does nothing to strengthen the Democratic ticket in 2024.

Theoretically, if Biden were to replace Harris on the ticket with a young and dynamic leader, he could strengthen the ticket and the Democrats' chances of winning the elections in November, 2024.

But because Biden is a stubborn and willful old man, this could only happen if there were a concerted rebellion among the Democratic ranks in the Senate and in the House, and possibly among the major contributors in the Democratic donor class.

Given their track record, this is not a likely scenario.

Yet is appears to be the only scenario which might lead to a Democratic victory in November.

Biden and his coterie cling to the belief that the very strong state of the economy, and other Biden successes, will as the campaign progresses convince voters that he is the better candidate.

In a rational world, that scenario might be possible.

In a world where voters had a memory, that scenario might be plausible.

But in America, a country that has no memory, that scenario is not likely.

We are not living in the United States, today, in a world of reason.

Rather, we are living in phantasmagoric times, in a world of Unreason governed by mass political emotions, as confirmed by the strength of Trump and the fascist movement which has taken over the Republican Party.

A historical comparison is apposite, and instructive.

At no point before 1933 did the outlook for Adolf Hitler and the fascists in Germany look as favorable as it does now for Donald Trump and the fascists in the United States.

Anything is possible, and the worst seems increasingly likely.

FURTHER READING

1. See, e..g,

1) Collins Concise English Dictionary © HarperCollins Publishers:

fascist /ˈfæʃɪst/ (sometimes capital) n

1. an adherent or practitioner of fascism

2. any person regarded as having right-wing authoritarian views

adj

Also: fascistic /fəˈʃɪstɪk/

   1. characteristic of or relating to fascism

2) Collins Concise English Dictionary © HarperCollins Publishers::

fascism /ˈfæʃɪzəm/n (sometimes capital)

   1. any ideology or movement inspired by Italian Fascism, such as German National Socialism; any right-wing nationalist ideology or movement with an authoritarian and hierarchical structure that is fundamentally opposed to democracy and liberalism

   2. any ideology, movement, programme, tendency, etc, that may be characterized as right-wing, chauvinist, authoritarian, etc

   3. prejudice in relation to the subject specified: body fascism

Etymology: 20th Century: from Italian fascismo, from fascio political group, from Latin fascis bundle; see fasces

2. Neil Postman, quoting Bill Moyers, in Amusing ourselves to Death: Public Discourse in the age of Show Business, Random House, 1985, Penguin Books, 1986, 2006), p. 137.

30

May 11, 2024

A Writer's Doubt

Personal Note

The world is so vast, itself but an atom in an immensely vaster Universe. But whatever the significance of our writing in the grand scheme of things, it could theoretically be significant for the flesh and blood human beings who inhabit our time snd space on this planet.

I have contributed my knowledge and reasoned analysis to discourse about world events. But my voice is tiny, and seems to have little or no influence on major decisions and world affairs.

I write for those whose ears are tuned to Reason, and who have some awareness of the wider world beyond the borders of the United States.

I write in parallel with the efforts of countless others who, like me, hope that reason and a knowledge of history and international law will have some bearing on decisions and the course of events.

In the United States, those of similar bent are now a small minority. According to recent polls, younger Americans have ranked foreign policy issues as of much less concern than have older generations.

Leading Republicans say they will not necessarily accept the results of the elections in November if their candidate does not win.

What is the point of writing and analyzing political developments and government decisions based on the facts, relevant history, and international law?

What is the value of pointing out that Trump and the Republicans represent a fascist movement which could take over the government of the United States? And if they do, that Trump could try to help Putin and the Russians win their war against Ukraine?

I guess the point is the same as it has always been. The voice of Reason, however weak it may become, must never be silenced.

I can do very little. But what I can do is add to the chorus of Reason which while perhaps weak now may become stronger in the future.

Mine is but one voice. A weak human voice. The hope, however, is that it will help inspire the voices of others. Until one day, as Martin Luther King said in his "I have a dream speech" in 1963,

"Justice (will) roll down like waters, and righteousness like an ever-flowing stream." (King was quoting Amos: 5:24 from the Bible.)

The demand for Justice has been constant throughout recent history.

The demand for Freedom has grown since the 20th century, and its guarantee is now enshrined in countless international human rights treaties and constitutions.

The demand for Law and International Law has grown steadily since the early twentieth century, and the response is now established in many constitutions and in the United Nations Charter and innumerable international treaties and conventions.

The demand for Peace has existed for thousands of years.

We raise our voice in defense of Reason, and of the spiritual values of Freedom, Justice, Law, and Peace.

We hope to inspire other voices, in a small way, and that these voices will help lead us back to a world of Reason, where all good men and women can join hands in the struggle for Freedom, Justice, Law, and Peace.

Naive? Perhaps. But what is the alternative?

Simple. Important. All important.

But even lonely voices need encouragement. Feedback. Support. Examples of how others are pursuing these goals.

31

June 14, 2024

Alvin Bragg and other New American Heroes

News reporting moves on. Let us not forget these heroes.

I t is highly fitting and perhaps deeply symbolic that 163 years after the beginning of the Civil War, Alvin Bragg. a son of Harlem and a son of Harvard, has now passed into the pantheon of American heroes, along with Judge Juan Merchan and the 12 jurors who on May 30, 2024 found Donald Trump guilty of all 34 felonies for which he was being tried.

Together they may have struck the blow that will mark the turning point in American history in the struggle to save the Constitution and the Republic from the fascist challenge represented by Donald Trump and his followers.

Of course, the brave and dedicated lawyers who prosecuted the case in a Manhattan district court, as well as the court's personnel, also deserve their rightful place in the history books.

Judge Juan Merchan, who conducted the Manhattan trial fairly and with great skill, and the 12 anonymous jurors deserve their rightful place in the pantheon of American heroes. Despite outrageous attacks from Donald Trump and his supporters, and thinly veiled threats of physical violence, these ordinary American citizens just did their jobs.

Fanny Willis, the courageous prosecutor in Atlanta who obtained the 41 indictments against Trump and his 18 co-conspirators in their attempt to overthrow the 2020 presidential election, also deserves her place among these American heroes.

Nathan Wade, the chief prosecutor in the Georgia case until he was forced to resign as a result of revelations about his affair with Willis beginning in late 2021 (after he was hired), also deserves great credit for his able management of the indictments and plea agreements with some of the accused, in a very complicated case.

The fact that he and Willis had an affair merely demonstrates that they are human, and that even human beings with flaws can perform their jobs with courage and rectitude. No evidence of impropriety in their conduct of the proceedings against Trump and his co-conspirators has emerged.

Willis and Wade are black, as is Alvin Bragg, which may account for some of the vitriol and threats of violence, including death threats, which have been directed against them. To their credit, they demonstrated great bravery in performing their jobs despite these threats.

These new American heroes are showing us and the world the way the American justice system, based on the rule of law and the jury system, is supposed to work—even in critical cases against high-profile and powerful defendants.

Trump and his supporters decry the fact that he is the first American president to have been indicted and convicted of felonies. These, however, were of great significance because they were committed in furtherance of a conspiracy to overthrow the 2020 presidential election and with it the Constitution of the United States.

Trump has succeeded in corrupting part of the federal justice system, with his appointment of three r ultra-conservative members to the Supreme Court which now has a right-wing majority which has made it a rogue Court. It is a Court that is out of control, and apparently willing to throw precedent to the wind and to abandon traditional precepts of constitutional interpretationq. Beyond the *Dobbs* decision overthrowing *Roe v. Wade*, the justices have acted to delay the criminal trials of Donald Trump by accepting an appeal of the case in which he claims absolute presidential immunity, when they might easily have simply let the lower Court of Appeals decision stand.

Most significantly, the right-wing majority of the Supreme Court appears to have swayed even the liberal members of the Court to join in reading Section 3 of the 14th Amendment out of the Constitution, by holding, on the most spurious of rationales. that its plain text and clear historical background simply do not apply. Leading constitutional scholars and judges, both conservative and liberal, both Republican and Democratic, have expressed the clear view that Section 3 *does* apply, and that because Donald Trump engaged in or supported the insurrection that culminated on January 6, 2021—as held as a matter of fact by the trial court---he should be barred from ever holding federal or state office.

Had the Supreme Court justices upheld the clear text of the Constitution, we would not be faced with the prospect of a convicted felon running for the presidency and the distinct possibility that he might win the November 5, 2024 election.

Trump has also appointed lower-level judges who have gone out of their way to assist him in delaying his criminal trials or in other ways. Judge Aileen Cannon in the U.S. District Court for Southern Florida has leaned over backwards in her rulings to delay the trial of Donald Trump in the case involving his alleged illegal retention of highly classified documents, including some relating to U.S. nuclear secrets.

U.S. Special Prosecutor Jack Smith has done an admirable job in securing grand jury indictments in the classified documents case in Southern Florida, and also in the January 6 insurrection case being tried in Washington. D.C. But he cannot make up for the fact that Attorney General Merrick Garland delayed for almost two years the naming of a Special Prosecutor who would energetically pursue the investigation and indictment of Trump. Had Garland acted with dispatch, juries in Trump's trials would probably have reached their verdicts by now.

What Trump's conviction on May 30, 2024 strongly suggests is that he will be found guilty of most if not all of the very serious felonies for which he has been indicted and which remain to be tried before a jury.

Not only is Donald Trump the first likely presidential candidate to be a convicted felon, *for crimes related to electoral fraud,* but he is also the first president who appears to have been on a massive crime spree—like crimes spewing out of a fire hose--before, during, and after his term in office.

We may assume, given the amount of publicly available evidence and the detailed charges and evidence outlined in Trump's various felony indictments, as well as evidence gathered by the House Select January 6 Committee, that he is guilty of the crimes with which he has been charged by grand juries in Washington, Miami, and Atlanta.

To be sure, the standard of proof for convicting and potentially incarcerating an accused derendant is "proof beyond a reasonable doubt". That standard does not apply, however, to forming political judgments about the conduct of a candidate for high political office.

There is nothing in our Constitution or laws, or in common sense, that says a candidate for the nation's highest public office must not be judged unqualified unless he meets the highest standard of evidence for a criminal conviction, "proof beyond a reasonable doubt".

Moreover, Donald Trump has satisfied even that high standard, having been convicted by a jury on May 30 of 34 felonies.

We owe the deepest debt of gratitude to these new American heroes, these servants of the law who in the face of death threats and physical threats to themselves, their families, and their staffs have demonstrated uncommon courage and dedication to upholding the rule of law in America.

If the fascist threat represented by Trump and today's Republican Party is defeated in the November 5, 2024 elections, as now seems more possible if not likely than it did prior to Trump's conviction on May 30 , these conscientious citizens who acted with courage to uphold the rule of law will go down in history as having marked a turning point that ended up saving the Republic.

We are witnessing the final stages of the death of the Republican Party A new party or parties will now arise to take its place. There is no room in America for a party of fascism which rejects the Constitution and the Rule of Law.

These new American heroes have done their part to ensure, in the words of Abraham Lincoln in his Gettysburg Address, "that government of the people, by the people, for the people, shall not perish from the earth."

32

July 11, 2024

The Democrats' Winning Team is on the Bench

Following President Joe Biden's disastrous performance in the presidential debate on June 27, 2024 and his failure to ease doubts in his interview on ABC with George Stephanopoulos on July 5, Democratic panic over Biden's candidacy for the presidency has only grown.

Democratic leaders have voiced grave concern in private, but hidden behind the oft-repeated mantra that it is up to Joe Biden to decide whether to withdraw from the race.

That is like saying that a drunken steamboat captain who is steering the boat towards a waterfall has the sole power of decision over whether he should yield the ship's wheel to the first mate or someone else who is sober. Instead, the passengers, whose deaths become more probable each minute as the steamboat approaches the waterfall, need to rush the captain and wrest the ship's wheel from his drunken grasp.

We in America face a similar moment, as Joe Biden threatens to take the steamboat of America over the waterfall that leads to a Trump victory in November, and the triumph of the fascist movement led by Trump and the pro-Russian Republican Party that believe in neither democracy nor the rule of law.

Democrats, like the the passengers on the steamboat, need to rush President Biden and seize the Democratic ticket from the death grip of a vain and stubborn old man with diminishing mental faculties.

One obstacle holding them back has been widespread uncertainty about who could replace Biden and Kamala Harris on the ticket.

The answer has been sitting on the bench and hiding in plain sight,

Gavin Newsom and Gretchen Whitmer, two governors of large and important states, would make up a powerful Democratic ticket that could blow Trump put of the water, and along with him Republican candidates for the House and the Senate.

Newsom and Whitmer could lead the Democrats to a landslide in the presidential election, retention of and even gains in the Senate, and a large majority in the House.

Gavin Newsom (b. 1967) has served as governor of California since 2019, Previously, he was Lieutenant Governor from 2011 to 2019, and Mayor of San Francisco from 2004 to 2011.

Newsom is handsome, charming, hihgly intelligent, and extremely well-spoken. He is governor of a state with 39 million people and the fifth largest exonomy in the world. If it were a country, California would be the 36th most populous nation in the world. He also has international experience of the kind that is sorely needed in thecWhite House.

Gretchen Whitmer (b. 1971) has served as governor of Michigan since 2019. She served in the Michigan House of Representatives[110] from 2001 to 2006 and in the Michigan Senate[111] from 2006 to 2015.

She won reelection as governor in 2022 by a margin of some 11 points. With Michigan and Wisconsin being among the seven swing states that will be critical in the Noveber, 2024 elections, she would add significant electoral strengh to the Democratic ticket.

Will the Democrats rush the drunken steamboat captain and wrest control of the ship's wheel from his stubborn and determined grasp? Will they nominate Newsom and Whitmer to be their candidates on the

Democratic ticket? This would be a powerful ticket that could lead to a Democratic sweep in 3024.

The future of democracy in America and of a civilization based on the U.N. Charter-based international legal order may depend on the answers to these questions.

33

July 16, 2024

Biden Can't Win.
Can Democrats Avoid Defeat?

BACKGROUND

See,

(1) Michael S. Schmidt and Mark Mazzetti, "Schiff Warned of Wipeout for Democrats if Biden Remains in Race; Representative Adam B. Schiff of California told attendees at a Democratic fund-raiser that the party would lose the Senate and miss a chance to take the House if the president did not drop out," New York Times, July 16, 2924 (10:32 a.m. ET).[112]

(2) Doug Sosnik,"Biden's Path to Re-election Has All But Vanished," Washington Post, July 12, 2024[113] (Graphics by Quoctrung Bui). *Mr. Sosnik was a senior adviser to President Bill Clinton from 1994 to 2000 and has advised over 50 governors and U.S. senators.*

(3) James Rowles, "Gavin Newson and Gretchen Whitmer: The Democrats' winning ticket is sitting on the bench," Trenchant Observations, July 11,2024.[114]

(4); Peggy Noonan, "Biden Can't Spin His Way Out of This; The president's handlers think he can plow ahead, but his position will only get worse. What a tragedy," Wall Street Journal, July 3, 2024 (5:27 pm).[115]

On July 12, 2024, Doug Sosnik published a fascinating op-ed piece in the Washington Post. In it Sosnik demonstrated persuasively, with poll numbers and charts of historical trends, why it is extremely unlikely that Joe Biden can win the presidential election on November 5, 2024.

Meanwhile, Schmidt and Mazzetti of the *New York Times* reported that Rep. Adam Schiff (D-CA) had raised the critical questions about Biden's continued candidacy at a fundraiser in the Hamptons. They wrote:

Representative Adam B. Schiff, the California Democrat who is running for Senate, warned during a private meeting with donors on Saturday that his party was likely to suffer overwhelming losses in November if President Biden remained at the top of the ticket, according to two people with direct knowledge of Mr. Schiff's remarks at the meeting.

If Mr. Biden remained, not only would he lose to former President Donald J. Trump, he could be enough of a drag on other Democratic candidates that the party would most likely lose the Senate and miss an opportunity to win control of the House, Mr. Schiff said at a fund-raiser in New York.

"I think if he is our nominee, I think we lose," Mr. Schiff said during the meeting, according to a person with access to a transcription of a recording of the event. "And we may very, very well lose the Senate and lose our chance to take back the House.

Schiff, a leading Democrat in the House, currently has a wide lead in his race for a Senate seat in California.

Joe Biden is in total denial regarding his poor chances in November and the grave concerns which exist among Democrats following his disastrous performance in the presidential debate with Donald Trump on May 27, 2024.

He does have supporters. Among the strongest are Donald Trump and leaders in the Republican Party, who obviously think he will be easiest Democratic candidate to beat.

As Schiff asserted, the elections in November are about much more than whether Biden wins reelection and defeats Trump.

It is possible that Biden could eke out a narrow victory over Trump, but America could still lose.

If the Republicans win the Senate, they will be able to block Biden nominations to the Supreme Cour, leaving the current right-wing majority in control.

If the Republicans win the Senate and the presidency, they might be able to appoint several more right-wing ideologues to the Supreme Court increasing the prospects that the present rogue Supreme Court will continue to thwart Democratic initiatives and to turn the Constitution on its head.

The Court has demonstrated that it is the firm control of a right-wing extremist majority in three important recent decisions.

First, in *Dobbs v. Jackson* (June 24, 2022), the Court overthrew *Roe v. Wade* (January 22, 1973) and the constitutional right to abortion, jettisoning some 50 years of constitutional jurisprudence.

In the second decision, *Trump v. Anderson* (March 4, 2024), the Court read Section 3 of the 14th Amendment out of the Constitution. In that case, the U.S. Supreme Court reversed a decision by the Colorado Supreme Court upholding the finding by a Colorado jury that Donald Trump had supported an insurrection and that under the specific language of Section 3 and state law he could not hold any federal or state elected office.

As it did in *Bush v. Gore* in 2000, the Supreme Court ignored precedents holding that it should defer to state supreme court decisions interpreting state law, here the law regulating who can be on the ballot.

The principal limitation on this principle is if the case involves the violation of a U.S. constitutional right. In *Bush v. Gore (2000)* the Court invented one, never mentioned before and never to be cited as precedent in the future, in order to hand the presidency to George W, Bush.

In *Trump v. Anderson*, by reading paragraph 3 of the 14th Amendment out of the Constitution, the Court allowed Donald Trump to appear on the Colorado ballot and in effect on ballots throughout the country.

It is hard to fathom why the three liberal justices on the Court went along with the majority opinion. Perhaps they were afraid of the consequences in the street if they banned Trump from the ballot. As a matter of constitutional law, their acquiescence with the decision of the majority was a blatant abdication of their duty to uphold the Constitution.

Leading constitutional scholars and former judges, both liberal and conservative, both Democratic and Republican, were firmly of the view that Section 3 applied to Trump and that he should be barred from the ballot. The legislative history and contemporary understanding of the reach of Section 3 when the 14th Amendment was ratified by the states clearly supported the conclusion that Section 3 was intended to apply to a case like that of Trump.

The third decision addressed the question of presidential immunity from prosecution. In *Trump v. United Stares* (July 1, 2024), the Supreme Court overruled a decision by a federal court of appeals, and held instead that the president is entitled to immunity from prosecution for any of his official acts, leaving it to the lower courts, and ultimately to the U.S. Supreme Court, to decide what actions were official acts. Moreover, tbe Court went even further, holding that evidence related to the president's official acts could not be used by the prosecution in a criminal case even when the president was being prosecuted for non-official acts.

By holding that, in practical effect, the president is above the law, the Court opened the door to establishment of a dictatorship in the United States.

The immediate effect of the Court's decision has been to delay the prosecution of Trump for the federal crimes for which he has been indicted in Washington.D.C. (the January 6 case), and in Miami, Florida (the classified documents case).

Further complicating matters, on July 15, 2024, Judge Aileen Cannon in Miami dismissed the classified documents case, on the ground that the Special Prosecutor, Jack Smith, had improperly brought the case because he had not been confirmed by the Senate. Her decision flew in the face of 25:years of settled precedent and Justice Department practice, even under President Trump. Smith will appeal the decision to the 11th Circuit Court of Appeals.

The Supreme Court's immunity decision in *Trump v. United States* has even given Trump's lawyers in the Stormy Daniels hash money case, in a New York state court, grounds for appeal and an extended delay in Trump's sentencing for the 34 felonies for which a Manhattan jury found him guilty on May 30, 2024,

The November elections will determine whether Trump can further guarantee control by a right-wing extremist majority of the Supreme Court, for the rest of our lifetimes, or whether the Democrats can win the presidency, retain the Senate, win back the House, and adopt legislation that would expand the membership of the Court.

Should the Democrats win both houses and the presidency, it might then be possible for them to increase the number of justices on the Supreme Court, in a manner which restores balance to the Court's interpretation of the Constitution.

In short, one of the biggest stakes in tbe November elections will be who controls the Supreme Court for the rest of our lives.

Second, the outcome of the November elections is likely to determine whether the United States continues to support Ukraine with military and economic aid, and whether it continues to lead the Atlantic Alliance (NATO) in opposing Russian aggression in Ukraine, thereby upholding international law and the U.N. Charter-based international legal order.

If Trump wins, the future of Ukraine will be placed gravely in doubt.

If Republicans retain control of the House, further aid for Ukraine is unlikely to be approved, or even if approved is likely to be greatly reduced.

We should not be stupid.

Viktor Orban of Hungary recently visited Trump in Mar-a-Lago. He then visited Vladimir Putin in Moscow, before subsequently visiting Xi Jinping in Beijing. On Monday, July 15, Trump chose Senator J.D. Vance to be his vice-presidential candidate. Vance has been an adamant opponent aid to Ukraine.

The pro-Russian Republican Party is no longer the party of Abraham Lincoln, Theodore Roosevelt, Dwight Eisenhower, Ronald Reagan, and George Herbert Walker Bush. It has become the party of the fascist movement in the United States led by Donald Trump.

Even if Biden ekes out a narrow victory, America could lose if the Republicans win the Senate and the House, or just the House.

It appears very clear that Biden can't win, and that if he proceeds with his candidacy the Democrats may lose both the Senate and the House.

The question for the Democrats, therefore, and particularly for those up for election, is whether they can avoid defeat.

The only path for the Democrats to pursue to avoid defeat in the Senate and the House would appear to be replacing Joe Biden with a more viable candidate.

Vice president Kamala Harris might have better chances to eke out a narrow victory than does Biden.

But she is not a strong candidate in her own right. Strategists should remember how she failed to gain traction in the Democratic primaries in 2020. Voters didn't like her. She would be unlikely to win the nomination in an open primary. She owes her position as vice president to Congressman Jim Clyburn (D-S.C.) and to the identity politics of the Democratic Party.

However, the November elections are not likely to be won on the basis of the identity politics of the Democratic Party.Given the stakes in the elections, and we have mentioned only the most obvious, the Democrats need to select the strongest possible ticket, and not merely aim at eking out a narrow presidential victory while losing the Senate and/or the House.

They need to put together a ticket that will blow Trump and his pro-Russian Republican supporters out of the water.

The opportunity for the Democrats is there, to not only avoid defeat but to resoundingly vanquish the candidates of Trump's pro-Russian Republican Party, while at the same time dealing a mortal blow to the American fascist movement he leads.

As we have noted, such a winning ticket is sitting on the bench in the persons of Gavin Newsom and Gretchen Whutmer, the governors of California and Michigan respectively.

If the Democrats can use their imagination and name Newsom and Whitmer to the ticket, these might lead a successful crusade that rids the country of the curse of Donald Trump and the cancer on the body politic represented by him and his supporters.

That would be a campaign of hope, looking to the future. It should find a receptive audience among Americans who are tired of constant drama and anger, and who are looking for hope and the promise of a calmer, brighter future.

34

July 19, 2024

Biden's Stubborn Ambition Puts Democracy and the World at Great Risk.

Name me a foreign leader who thinks I'm not the most effective leader in the world on foreign policy," Mr. Biden said, adding, "Tell me who the hell that is." [116]

President Joe Biden has become delusional and, like Trump, believes only he can save the country and the world.

Like Trump, he manifests a narcissism so great that it is a threat to American democracy.

If he stays in the race, Biden is extremely likely to usher in government by Trump and his fascist supporters, and be the cause of crushing Democratic losses to the Republicans in both the Senate and the House.

The sheer hubris of the man is mind-boggling. He is doing everything he can to cling to the nomination in a desperate effort to hold on to power.

He thinks the election is about him, and not about the future of democracy in the United States, and U.S. leadership in the struggle to defend Ukraine against Russian aggression and to uphold the U.N. Charter-based international legal order.

145

He and his retinue argue that he has done a great job as president since 2021, despite what is arguably the worst foreign policy record since World War II, and domestic failures such as not investigating and prosecuting Trump and his accomplices for nearly two years.

Most scholars and experts, horrified at Donald Trump and fearful of hurting Democratic prospects in elections, have refrained from any sustained and cold-eyed criticism of Biden and his policies. Many work as consultants to government officials and on government projects. Their reticence is perhaps understandable, though one wonders what it would take for them to take a stand.

In the foreign policy arena, at least, we have been a notable exception. We have excoriated Biden and his weak foreign policy team for a number of strategic errors, including in particular his decision in 2021 to withdraw all American military forces and contractors from Afghanistan.

With the Afghanistan withdrawal, Biden not only abandoned some 40 million Afghans to a cruel fate under medieval religious zealots known as the Taliban, but also abandoned 20 million Afghan girls and women to a harsh life of utter oppression by men under a regime which will not let them go to school, study at the university, or do professional work. Indeed, they cannot even leave their homes unless escorted by a male relative.

Biden asserted that none of his advisers had opposed the withdrawal, despite the fact that U.S. military leaders had firmly opposed his decision to withdraw. On this point, Biden repeatedly lied.

Even those urging Biden to withdraw from seeking the Democratic nomination routinely assert the decision is solely his to make. This may be true under the bureaucratic rules of the Democratic National Committee and certain state laws. These presumably can be changed. Whether they would require electors to vote for an individual in obvious declining health, including mental faculties, is an interesting question.

Everyone is singing Biden's praises as they seek to coax him into surrendering his death grip on the nomination. One is reminded of a quip by Will Rogers who once said,

Diplomacy is the art of saying 'Nice doggie' until you can find a rock.

Democratic leaders are currently engaged in the kind of delicate diplomacy Will Rogers would readily understand.

35

August 11, 2024

Trump is Increasingly Delusional and out of Touch with Reality

If media will report the truth, a generational shift away from the Republican Party could occur

Tom Nichols in an eye-opening article *The Atlantic*[117] reports on Donald Trump's press conference on May 8 at Mar-a-Lago, and sharply criticizes the *New York Times* and the *Washington Post* for failing to report the reality of what actually happened at the press conference.[118]

Nichols writes that a more accurate account of the news conference might read as follows:

> The former president, lying about abortion laws, said women murder their own babies in the delivery room. He megalomaniacally claimed that he gets bigger crowds than anyone in history, and compared himself to Martin Luther King Jr. He descended into fantasy by telling a story about surviving a helicopter emergency that never happened with a man who wasn't there.

Should the reality of Donald Trump's current state of mind and mental health ever penetrate the bubble of Republican propaganda, it is possible that the Republicans could suffer a defeat at the polls in November of historic proportions.

FURTHER READING

See Jennufer Rubin, "Trump's decline: His interviews and lies get worse; as the 2024 race draws tighter, the former president's actions suggest he is spiraling." Washington Post, August 16, 2024 (9:00 am EDT).[119]

Part Eight

Gladiatorial Combat. Trump and Nazi Propaganda, and Immigration as the Decisive Issue in the 2024 Campaign

36

September 24, 2024

Numb

BACKGROUND

See,

James Rowles, "Sleepwalking in the garden of fascism: 'Merrily we roll along!" The Trenchant Observer, June 2, 2021.[120]

Things are not going well in America or in the world.
Like many others, I am numb.

I am numb from seeing Israel commit war crimes on a daily basis in Gaza, and acquiescing in if not fomenting settler violence in the West Bank.

I am numb from observing America's complicity in the commission of these Israeli war crimes.

I am numb from all of Joe Biden's talk of peace in Gaza and Israel, coupled with his absolute refusal to use the instruments of American power to bring about that peace.

I am numb from all of the talk about a ceasefire and release of Israeli hostages deal, the evil ploy used by Israel to hold out hope while it continues to kill thousands of civilians in Gaza, and while Benjamin Netanyahu deliberately acts to kill any ceasefire and release of hostages deal whenever negotiations appear close to agreement.

I am tired of Joe Biden's endless assertions that he is pressuring Israel to kill fewer civilians, as he approves a $20 billion military aid package without effective limits on Israeli actions, without even emphasizing those restrictions already contained in American law which prohibit arms transfers when the arms might be used in ways other than self-defense (as defined by international law and the U.N. Charter).

I am numb from watching the horror show in Gaza, and the horror show in the White House where the president will not withhold the U.S. veto in the U.N. Security Council to allow it to take effective action by, e.g., imposing sanctions on Israel for its blockade and other war crimes in Gaza.

I am numb from watching Joe Biden impose prohibitions on the use by Ukraine of weapons supplied by NATO countries against targets in Russia when such action is fully justified under the international law of self-defense and the United Nations Charter.

I am numb from listening to specious justifications for such restrictions, with the armchair warriors in U.S. military ranks telling the Ukrainians the weapons would not be effective despite Ukraine's contrary view and urgent and repeated pleas for such weapons.

I am numb from observing Joe Biden's cowardice in confronting Vladimir Putin and Russia since the Russian invasion of Ukraine in February, 2022, always withholding needed weapons for as long as he can until unity in the NATO alliance threatens to dissolve.

I am numb from the cowardice that assumes that this is Ukraine's war, not *our* war, as the world faces the greatest challenge to civilization and the international legal order since World War II.

Finally, I am numb as I watch half the people in America abandon reason and all moral principles as they surrender to the cult of Donald Trump and the growing fascist movement in the United States.

I am numb as I see the formation of a powerful alliance between so-called "low-information voters" and highly educated business people, often billionaires or very wealthy individuals, who cynically support the Leader believing as their counterparts in Germany believed in the 1930's that they can control the fascists.

Who are these "low-information voters"? They are the voters who with their cynical business allies would again elect Donald Trump, who charitably might be called the ultimate "low information president".

Yet let us dig further. What, really, is a "low-information voter"?

He is a voter who has not taken the trouble to investigate the facts regarding different candidates and issues, being content to go with the mass emotions of his tribe.

Is it not the first duty of citizenship in a democracy to inform oneself about the candidates and the issues in an election?

The media will not call out these "low-information voters" as lazy or stupid people, because they depend on selling soap and other goods and services to these same people.

Who came up with such a marvelous euphemism as the "low-information voter"?

Well, I'm numb from all of the above.

One thing is clear to me.

The future of American democracy, as well as the moral basis and strategic coherence of U.S. foreign policy, now depends on the half of the American electorate who might still be able to think and act in a rational manner, if they could only wake up from the their current torpor and numbness, and *act* to save the Republic.

FURTHER READING

James Rowles, "A Parable of our time: 'Our democratic house is on fire!'" The Trenchant Observer, September 23, 2021.[121]

37

September 6, 2024

Gladiatorial Combat

America's political circus pits honorable sitting Vice-President against a convicted felon being tried for multiple felonies in Washington, Atlanta, and Miami

On some great and glorious day the folks of the land will reach their heart's desire at last and the White House will be adorned by a downright moron.
–H.L. Mencken,[122] *"The Baltimore Sun, July 26, 1920*

That day took place in January 2017 after the American people elected Donald Trump to be President of the United States.

Mencken was right. As Secretary of State Rex Tillerson reportedly blurted out to colleagues as he exited his first major meeting with Trump, "The man's a fucking moron."

But he is a particularly dangerous moron, a convicted felon who led a conspiracy and attempt to overthrow the 2020 presidential election and with it the Constitution, and the Leader of an American fascist movement which today seeks to take over the presidency and undermine the rule of law in the world's oldest living democracy.

On Trump's crimes, *see,*

Melissa Murray and Andrew Weissmann, *The Trump Indictments; The Historic Charging Documents With Commentary* (New York: W.H. Norton & Company, 2024).

On May 30, 2024, in a New York state court in Manhattan, Trump was convicted by a jury of 12 anonymous men and women of 34 felonies related to a hush money payment to Stormy Daniels made through Michael Cohen and fraudulent bookkeeping entries made to cover up reimbursement of the payment by Cohen.

How did America come to this point, in which a Vice-President of the United States, a fomer U.S Senator, and a former Attorney General of California, with an unblemished ethical record as an elected official, is constrained to enter into a modern-day gladiatorial contest with a dangerous convicted felon in order to pursue the presidency in November, 2024?

One is reminded of the title of Gary Sick's book on the failed Iranian hostages rescue attempt in 1979, *All Fall Down* (New York: Random House, 1985). Indeed, it seems that many sectors of society and many leaders have contributed to the deterioration in our political system which has taken it to its present nadir.

It is at such a low point that a gladiatorial battle between the two principal candidates seeking election to the presidency will be judged by voters in part on how well the candidates perform as gladiators in this combat. The contest will be viewed or read about by voters who may decide the outcome of the November 5, 2024 election.

In reporting on this match-up the media completely ignore the context and treat the battle as if were between two reputable candidates. It is not. They will continue to ignore this context during and in the days and months after the debate.

Rational voters will largely ignore how the two gladiators perform, but won't ignore the analytical conclusions that should be drawn about the character and crimes of the the convicted felon who is campaigning to become president again.

The problem is that perhaps half the country and potential majorities in seven swing states do not fit within the category of rational voters dedicated to upholding democracy and the rule of law. Many are Trump cult followers and nothing can persuade them not to vote for the convicted felon.

Many others are wealthy businessmen who are willing to overlook deep character flaws and criminal behavior, including an utter disregard for the truth, disdain for legal constraints, and a troubling criminal record including a conspiracy to launch a coup d'état and an attempt to overthrow the Constitution.

Viewers who watch the gladiatorial contest on September 10 and voters who read about it in subsequent days should bear these facts and this context in mind.

The race for the presidency is not a horse race between two legitimate candidates. One is a career politician with with an unblemished record of years in public life.

The other is a convicted felon and the leader of a fascist movement which does not respect truth, the Constitution, or the rule of law.

These are the combatants in the gladiatorial duel scheduled to take place on television on September 10.

FURTHER READING

See James Rowles, "Public Discourse in America," Trenchant Observations, August 30, 2024.[123] Reproduced in the Introduction, above

38

September 21, 2024

The Brilliance of Trump's Propaganda and How to Counter It

"Illegal Haitian immigrants are stealing pet dogs
and cats and eating them in Springfield, Ohio"

BACKGROUND

See,

1) Kris Maher, Valerie Bauerlein, and Tawnell D. Hobbs, "How the Trump Campaign Ran With Rumors About Pet-Eating Migrants—After Being Told They Weren't True; Springfield, Ohio, city officials were contacted by Vance's team and said the claims were baseless. It didn't matter and now the town is in chaos. Wall Street Journal, September 18, 2024 (12:01 am ET);[124]

2) "Trump falsely claims Haitian migrants are eating pets in Ohio," CBS News (You Tube), September 10, 2024;[125]
3) "Vance defends spreading claims that Haitian migrants are eating pets," NPR. September 15, 2024 (12:54 PM ET).[126]

Intellectually we know that voters frequently vote on the basis of their emotions. In practice, however, the Democrats never seem to get that fundamental fact, and proceed as if voters decided who to vote for solely on the basis of rational analyses of what is in their self-interest.

The Republicans, and particularly Donald Trump and his campaign, on the other hand, assume the voters are stupid, have no memory, and don't vote on the basis of what is rationally in their best interests.

That is how we can understand the 2024 Republican presidential campaign, and the repeated charge that illegal (very black) Haitian immigrants are stealing pet dogs and cats and eating them in Springfield, Ohio.

The Democrats try to counter such obviously mendacious propaganda with rational arguments, missing the point that the real communication is taking place on a different level and in a different channel, one aimed directly at the emotions of susceptible voters.

The real Republican message, addressed to the subconscious of these voters, is the following:

1) The nation is being invaded and taken over by illegal aliens, who like these Haitians are very black and are essentially criminal barbarians who steal family pets and eat them;

2) These black and brown immigrants from all over the world are taking over your country, and will replace the white population as the Democrats open the floodgates to massive immigration of these barbarians. These include, as Donald Trump incessantly repeats at his campaign rallies, rapists, murderers and other criminals who are being let out of prison from places like the (the Democratic Republic of) the Congo in Africa so that they can emigrate to the U.S.; and

3) Only Donald Trump and the Republicans can protect you from these black and brown illegal immigrants and the invading hordes

for whom the Democrats are opening the borders in order to bring these (black and brown) barbarians into our (white) country. Boiled down to its essence, it sounds like this:

1) Black (and brown) barbarian immigrants are taking over the country;
2) Only Trump and the Republicans can protect you and keep this from happening.

The subconscious message is even simpler:

Immigrants = take over country; Trump = Protection

The calculation of Trump and the Republican propagandists is that when the voter enters the voting booth, if not long before, the primitive emotions associated with these words will dictate the voter's choice.

Doubling down on these cynical and outragious lies helps to fix these primitive ideas in the voter's subconscious. So however absurd they may appear to rational observers, they serve an important function in influencing voters to vote for Trump.

In countering such propaganda, Democrats should of course make the rational arguments to rebut such preposterous lies, but without believing that such arguments will by themselves carry the day.

Mush more effective with persuadable voters would be to add to the rational arguments and even give prominence to different arguments and messages aimed at voters' emotions. For example, in the present case, Democrats might prepare ads that include interviews with model Haitian immigrants and with Haitian children in Springfield. They might also urge journalists to include such interviews in their reporting.

These interviews should be buttressed by interviews with Springfield city, school, and church officials, including in particular those who are white, debunking the Republican lies about "illegal (very black) Haitian immigrants stealing and eating pet dogs and cats in Springfield".

These interviews might include the following elements:

1) Haitian immigrants showing to the camera documentary proof that they are legally in the country;
2) A succinct but cogent explanation, in the immigrants' own words, of why they fled Haiti and are seeking asylum in the United States. (See the reports of the Inter-American Commission on Human Rights cited below.)
3) Interviews with Haitian children about their personal experience with violence, hunger, etc. in their home country;
4) Interviews with Haitian children from Springfield holding their pets, talking about what they do with their pets, and talking about how good and safe Springfield is for their pets.

The above rebuttals might be included in two-minute television commercials. or better yet in longer paid programs (of 15 or 30 minutes each that allow viewers to feel that they have gotten to know the Haitians and Haitian children who have been interviewed.

The cynical Republican propaganda about Haitians eating stolen pet cats and dogs in Springfield offers the Democrats a magnificent opportunity to flip over the rock hiding the cynicism of Republican propaganda and to expose the ugly racism and xenophobia that lie beneath that rock to the harsh daylight of truth.

Such an ad or paid program could be used on the Internet and in media markets throughout the country. It would not have to be tailored to each race and each market, which would make it quite economical in comparative terms.

The Democrats need rapid reaction teams which could put up rebuttals such as that suggested above very quickly. Unfortunately, they seem to be extraordinarily slow in rebutting memes such as the "illegal Haitians eating stolen dogs and cats" fabrication. It often seems as if any response requires many approvals up the bureaucratic chain of command before any rebuttal is published. By then it is usually too late.

Moreover, Democrats fail to move beyond rational arguments to appeal to the emotions of precisely those individuals which Trump and the Republican propagandists are targeting.

$$* * *$$

On a personal note, as a senior staff attorney at the Inter-American Commission on Human Rights (IACHR) of the Organization of American States (OAS) and the lawyer in charge of Haiti at the Commission, I coordinated the logistical and staff work during the Commission's on-site visit to Haiti from August 16 through August 25, 1978.

See,

1) Inter-American Commission on Human Rights, Report on the Situation of Human Rights in Haiti, OEA/Ser.L/V/II.46 doc. 66 rev. 1, 13 December 1979[127] (Original: French);

2) Inter-American Commission on Human Rights, Report on the Situation of Human Rights in Haiti, OEA/Ser.L/V/II.,Doc. 358, August 30, 2022[128] (Original: español).

The 1922 Report describes recent conditions in Haiti of particular relevance to the Haitian immigrants in Springfield, Ohio who reportedly are legally in the U.S.

From my work on Haiti at the IACHR and during the Commission's onsite visit in 1978, I have gained a deep appreciation for the many decent Haitians who simply want to live a normal life, in a country with scarce natural resources and a dark history of violence and dictatorship. For detailed examples of conditions in Haiti, see the above reports of the IACHR.

I still recall the first day during the Commission's onsite visit in Haiti when the Commission received complaints from individuals who had been the victims of human rights violations. We were staying at the Villa Creole Hotel in Petionville. a wealthy part of the capital up in the hills overlooking the plain and the harbor below.

The staff of the hotel had doubled in the days before our arrival. A man in his early forties in a brown suit with polished brown shoes and no suitcase was staying in the room immediately above mine. The hotel staff warned us that the new staff were all state security agents. When members of the Commission's staff wanted to talk to each other, we waded out to the middle of the swimming pool to have confidential conversations.

At the entrance of the hotel, there were several state security agents monitoring the arrival of anyone who might testify to human rights violations before the Commission. That first day, we didn't know if anyone would have the courage to come and testify before the Commission.

I remember clearly the first complainant who came to testify, walking past the security agents at the entrance. As I recall, he was a school teacher. He told us that he had traveled five hours since early morning by bus from a town near the border with the Dominican Republic to give his testimony. "I don't know if I will be alive at the end of the day today, but I have seen things that I must report to the Commission," he said. He proceeded to give his statement.

After him, a stream of courageous individuals came forward to present their complaints and testify before the Commission.

Before our trip to the island, I had met in a safe house in Manhattan with the leader of the Haitian Communist Party and separately with the leading independent journalist in Haiti, Jean Dominique,[129] who was the owner of the only independent radio station in the country, *Radio Haiti-Inter.*

Jean Dominique helped put me in touch with many key independent political leaders and journalists in Haiti. The latter included the young investigative reporters from *Le Petit Samedi Soir,* who continued their courageous work even after one of their members was killed.

I remember when on one dark, rainy night, after traveling on an empty road in the mountains above Kenscoff, I met Jean Dominque as he stepped out of dark shadows with a flashlight, on a large estate at our pre-arranged meeting location. An intrepid international diplomat drove me to the safe house and back to my hotel. If he had been discovered, he would have been expelled from the country. Jean Dominque got out the word and had a lot to do with many courageous individuals coming forward to file their complaints before the Commission In Cap Haitien on the northern coast, another city we visited, no one came forward to file a complaint.

During our stay in Haiti, Jean Dominique took advantage of our presence and the political opening it made possible His radio program became increasingly audacious, as he read portions of the Inter-American Convention on Human Rights to his audience, and even aggressively interviewed members of congress about land issues and other sensitive matters.

Andrew Young, then U.S. Ambassador to the United Nations and former Executive Director of the Southern Christian Leadership Conference (SCLC) and close associate of Dr. Martin Luther King,Jr., had persuaded 'Baby Doc", the son of longtime strongman"Papa Doc" Duvalier, and the current dictator of Haiti, to ratify the American Convention on Human Rights and to invite the IACHR to conduct an onsite visit to the country. Jean Dominique took full advantage of the resultant opening.

The point of this digression is that, despite its troubled history, Haiti has always had its fair share of enormously talented and courageous people.1978 was a hopeful moment in the country's history. Since then,

Haiti has sunk into a cauldron of violence where at least until recently most of the capital was being ruled by violent criminal gangs. Many of the people in Haiti have fled the violence and some have ended up in Springfield, Ohio.

In addition to unmasking the ugly racism and xenophobia of Donald Trump and the Republican Party today, the cyncal lies of Trump and J.D. Vance about the Haitian immigrants in Springfield mark a despicable low point in American politics.

It is an absolute outrage that Dondald Trump and J.D. Vance have defamed the Haitian immigrants of Springfield. In denouncing the Haitians with unforgivable lies, Trump and Vance have made clear once again what vile hate lies within the hearts of the leaders of the American fascist movement, which has unfortunately taken control of the Republican Party.

39

September 24, 2024

SATIRE: Haitian Dogs Are Eating White People in Springfield, Ohio

BACKGROUD

See, e.g.,

1) Mick Evans"Springfield Ohio's Haitian community ready for attention to move elsewhere," Yahoo/News, September 23, 2024 (12:37 PM PDT);[130]

2) Kimberly Nordyke, "John Oliver Wonders How Donald Trump's Claims About Haitians Eating Cats Isn't 'Disqualifying'; The 'Last Week Tonight' host set up a clip from Trump's presidential debate with Kamala Harris by calling it an 'exceptional moment in American oratory'," The Hollywood Reporter, September 22, 2024 (9:21 p.m.);[131]

3) Nardis Haile, "John Oliver shreds JD Vance for perpetuating pet-eating myth," Salon/ (Yahoo News) September 23, 2024 (12:34 o.m.);[132]

Haitian immigrants in Springfield, Ohio have been accused by former President Donald Trump and Republican Vice-presidential candidate J.D. Vance of stealing pet dogs and cats and eating them.

Many of these Haitian immigrants have dogs and cats themselves. In Springfield, many Haitian immigrants have been the object of threats and abuse, which has caused the closing of schools and led to many bomb threats.

Haitian dogs, in response to these attacks on their owners, have launched a campaign to protect them by eating white people. While human meat is not at the top of the menu of Haitian dog cuisine, the dogs can eat human meat when they need to, and in fact many of them have found human meat tasty.

City officials are at a loss as to how to stop the Haitian dogs from eating white people. Some animal rights activists have been arguing that the dogs are acting in collective self-defense or, alternatively, in legal terms, in defense of others.

At the same time, local government resources are now being strained by nightly demonstrations in Springfield as in other cities across the nation by a new organization named "Cat ladies for Springfield Haitians".

The controversy has divided the Springfield community with jokes going around among Trump and Vance supporters such as the following:

Q: "Do you know why masses of Haitians are headed toward Seattle?"

A: "They have heard that in Seattle it is always raining cats and dogs."

Chaos reigns in Springfield. Federal and local officials are now consulting around the clock on how best to bring to a halt the present campaign of Haitian dogs eating white people.

40

October 7, 2024

Media Bias Against Harris.
CPR for the American Body Politic

A great deal of the news coverage about Kamala Harris reflects a deep innate bias against her.

The press doesn't know how to report on Trump. They don't know how to analyze crazy. And they or their young editors are not inclined to look beneath the surface to find out and report on what is going on under the hood, so io speak, at the deep subconscious level where voters' emotions will determine how they vote on November 5, 2024.

November 5 is the day of America's date with Destiny.

The bias that is an innate feature of their reporting is that they hold Kamala Harris up to comparison not to her actual opponent, Donald Trump, but rather to some idealized rational presidential candidate who exists only in their imagination.

Their comparisons of Harris' speeches, policies, or character are always against this illusory candidate of their imagination. Making such comparisons, they strive to show how brilliant they are analytically. Meanwhile, the necessary comparisons with the real candidate, Donald Trump, are never formulated and never presented to their readers and their listeners.

Reporting on what is really going on in the campaign is consequently absent from their newspaper articles and their television reports.

How do you report on crazy?

How do you report on Trump's policies when he has no policies, other than talking points that might occur to him or his advisors on any given day, at any given moment?

Kamala Harris might not be the best presidential candidate the Democrats could have produced. But given Joe Biden's stranglehold on the nomination process and his obstinate refusal to withdraw from the race until he was absolutely forced to do so, Harris was the only feasible candidate for the Democrats—at that moment in time.

With Harris the Democrats at least had a chane to win the presidential election and control of the Senate and the House. With Joe Biden, an increasingly senile candidate, they faced inevitable defeat in all three arenas.

Kamala Harris was the best *possible* candidate for the Democrats.

For press and television and other reporters, the central question is, and always has been, how does she stack up against Donald Trump and how do the Democratic candidates stack up against their Republican opponents?

How do they stack up against Crazy?

How do they stack up against the lying Republican candidates who are utterly under the thumb of the crazy, lying, and criminal Leader of their authoritarian party?

Let us be frank and call it what it is: a fascist party totally controlled by a fascist Leader, Donald Trump.

Crazy, surrounded by leaders of a would-be fascist government.

Ponder this: Neither Trump, nor vice-presidential candidate J.D. Vance, nor Republican House Leader Mike Johnson will admit publicly that the 2020 presidential race was won by Joe Biden. Nor will they admit that there was virtually no evidence of any significant fraud— none. This fact was confirmed by the decisions of all 62 courts in which Trump raised spurious claims of fraud without a shred of credible evidence.

Furthermore, these same Republican leaders will not commit to accepting the presidential election results in 2024 if Trump doesn't win.

It is past time that reporters started reporting on what is really going on in the 2024 elections, and on the true character and democratic commitment of candidates from each of the two parties.

Without a fearless and vibrant press, America seems to be in a political coma.

Who will administer CPR on the comatose American body politic, if not the press?

41

October 11, 2024

Republican Felon Alleges Invasion of U.S. By Immigrant Criminal Hordes

BACKGROUND

See,

1) Sabrina Rodriguez, "Trump amplifies falsehoods about immigrants in closing appeal; As his edge on the economy fades, the Republican nominee campaigned in Aurora, Colo., on Friday, promoting false claims about Venezuelan gangs taking over residential buildings there, Washington Post, October 11, 2024 (Updated at 5:18 p.m. EDT);[133]

2) James Rowles, "The secret brilliance of Trump's Republican propaganda and how to counter it: 'Illegal Haitian immigrants stealing pet dogs and cats and eating them in Springfield, Ohio'," Trenchant Observations, September 21, 2024;[134]

3) James Rowles, "SATIRE: Haitian Dogs Are Eating White People in Springfield, Ohio," October 24, 2024.[135]

Irony that escapes the Insurrectionists

It is unfortunate that insurrectionists lack a sense of irony and even a sense of humor.

Otherwise, they might appreciate the keen irony in Donald Trump's unfounded allegations that the country is being invaded by hordes of illegal criminal immigrants.

He alleges that illegal criminal gangs are taking over towns in the U.S. like Aurora, Colorado.

The irony is that criminals led by arch felon Donald Trump are indeed plotting to take over the country, starting with the White House and the Congress. They plan to take over either through elections or according to some reports by other means.

Trump seems to be a great follower of Adolf Hitlers's propaganda advice, set forth in stark terms in Volume One, Chapter VI of his testimonial, *Mein Kampf*, written in prison following his failed coup d'état, the 1923 beer hall Putsch in Munich.

See,

Adolf Hitler, *Mein Kampf* English ed.(New York: Houghton Mifflin,1943 Ralph Manheim transl.), pp. 176-186. First published in German in 1925.

In Chapter VI of Volume One (on "War Propaganda"), the author asks, "To whom should propaganda be addressed? To the scientifically trained intelligentsia or to the less educated masses?" He answers, "It must be addressed always and exclusively to the masses."

The receptivity of the great masses is very limited, their intelligence is small, but their power of forgetting is enormous, In consequence of these facts, all effective propaganda must be limited to a very few points and must harp on these in slogans until the last member of the public understands what you want him to understand by your slogan.

The propaganda approach of Donald Trump and his campaign is right out of Hitler's playbook.

In 10 short pages of *Mein Kampf* the author presents a brilliant analysis of propaganda that, in the real world, moves the masses.

Democrats, if they are to effectively counter such propaganda, must understand the playbook their opponents are using.

To see how these propaganda techniques are being applied by Trump, see the second article listed in the **BACKGROUND** section above.

Part Nine

Final Thoughts

42

October 18, 2025

The Voter's Pledge

There are so many issues where a rational analysis suggests a victory by Donald Trump in the election on November 5 would be a fateful disaster for America and for the world.

The realization hits that the presidential election may not be decided by the half of the electorate that is guided by rational considerations or followers of those who are guided by rational considerations.

Indeed, the outcome may be decided by the mass emotions whipped up by the fascist leader of the Republican Party, which has become a fascist party under the iron grip of Donald Trump.

The consequences of a Trump victory would be catastrophic.

In power again, Trump and his fascist supporters would be in position over the next four years to undermine the rule of law and to carry out a successful coup d'etat.

Internationally, Trump would have a devastating effect on the U.N. Charter-based international legal order. As Moscow's "man in Washington", Trump would be likely to undermine NATO and the support of NATO countries and other allies for Ukraine and resisting Russian military aggression, war crimes, and illegal acquisition of territory by military conquest.

The deterrence of China from invading Taiwan would be greatly weakened.

But these are rational considerations.

It remains to be seen, on November 5, 2024, whether reason will be swept aside, or rational considerations will prevail in the election of a new president and a new Congress.

As a student of German history and the Third Reich, I am deeply concerned that America may be sleepwalking into a fascist future. The elections on November 5, 2024 will be a kind of Rorschach test of who we are as a people. Are we a country with a fascist majority? Or do small "d" democrats who believe in the Constitution and the rule of law still hold sway?

The battle to defeat the fascist threat in America will not be finally settled by the elections on November 5, 2024, though they could have a very large impact on that outcome in the future.

One thing is certain. If Donald Trump loses, we will see a rerun of the attempt to overturn the election similar to the attempt made in 2020, with one big difference. This time the institutional framework and identity of offficials who certify the election results will have been altered to favor Trump as the result of Republican actions over the last four years. Consequently, the result could be different.

For undecided voters and voters leaning toward Trump, the hour of truth approaches. . It is indeed time to take the title of this book to heart

In waking up to their civic responsibility to study the issues and the candidates, they should be guided by The Voter's Pledge, set forth here:

The Voter's Pledge

I will vote for candidates who are honest,
I will vote for candidates who tell the truth,
I will vote for candidates who will serve as models for my children,
    for my grandchildren, and for future generations.

Every citizen should take this pledge. Friends should ask friends and others to take the pledge. And if anyone refuses to take the pledge, citizens should look that person directly in the eye and ask, "Why not?" And they should expect and demand an honest answer. And insist on a serious and honest answer.

43

October 24, 2024

62 Years Ago, the World Stood on the Brink of Nuclear Annihilation.

If Donald Trump Had Been President During the
Cuban Missile Crisis, Would We Still Be Here?

A powerful reminder of the stakes in the November 5 presidential election.

62 years ago, in October 1962, in the Cuban Missile Crisis, described by Robert F. Kennedy in his book, *Thirteen Days: A Memoir of the Cuban Missile Crisis*, 19th ed. (New York: W.W. Norton, 1999), the world came much closer to nuclear annihilation than most people realize.

See Graham T. Allison and Philip Zelikow, *Essence of Decision: Explaining the Cuban Missile Crisis*, 2nd ed. (New York: Longman, 1999).

Now would be a good time to read or reread these books, and to watch the movie, *Thirteen Days* (2000).

Every voter in the November 5, 2024 presidential election should ask himself or herself, "If Donald Trump had been president in 1962, would we still be here?"

There can be no more powerful reminder of the stakes in this election than this thought.

44

October 20, 2024

The Stakes in the 2024 Elections

For Americans, the overarching question in the elections is whether they will be governed by a president of integrity, a president who is honest, a president dedicated to truth, and a president dedicated to upholding the Constitution and the rule of law.

The evidence is in on Donald Trump. We know the answers to these questions if he is elected on November 5, 2024,

For the rest of the world, the stakes are of enormous importance. The main questions are:

1. Will the United States continue military and economic aid to Ukraine, at current or higher levels, to ensure that Russian aggression against Ukraine is not successful?

2. Will the United States exercise the international leadership necessary to defeat Russian aggression and barbarism and uphold international law including international humanitarian law (the law of war), the United Nations Charter, and the U.N. Charter-based international legal order.?[136]

3. Will the United States be a leading force within the United Nations to successfully overcome international challenges such as global warming and climate change, the proliferation of nuclear and other weapons of mass destruction, the need for regulation

and control of artificial intelligence, and prevention and defense against biological threats such as the coronavirus?

The answers to these questions will all depend on who is elected president on November 5, 2024.

A recent book by Régis Genté, *Notre homme à Washington, Trump dans la main des Russes* (Paris: Editions Grasset, October 15, 2024), makes an overwhelming case that Donald Trump is in the hands of the Russians and indeed their "Man in Washington". Genté, an expert on Eastern Europe and the countries of the former Soviet Union and longtime correspondent of *Le Figaro* resident in Tbilisi, Georgia, has pulled together a massive amount of evidence that demonstrates beyond the slightest doubt that Moscow has been cultivating Trump for some four decades. The book helps the reader understand why Trump has never criticized Vladimir Putin and has over the years acted consistently to further Soviet and now Russian interests.

The elections on November 5 will amount to a national Rorschach test which will reveal who, in 2024, we Americans really are.

Are we fascists and willing to elect a fascist leader of a fascist Republican Party whose members do not believe in the rule of law and the maintenance of democracy?[137]

Or are we still, if only by a narrow margin, patriots dedicated to "the great task remaining before us" as set forth by Abraham Lincoln in his Gettysburg Address, in the following words?

Four score and seven years ago our fathers brought forth on this continent a new nation, conceived in liberty, and dedicated to the proposition that all men are created equal. Now we are engaged in a great civil war, testing whether that nation, or any nation so conceived and so dedicated, can long endure. We are met on a great battlefield of that war. We have come to dedicate a portion

of that field as a final resting place for those who here gave their lives that that nation might live. It is altogether fitting and proper that we should do this. But in a larger sense we cannot dedicate, we cannot consecrate, we cannot hallow this ground. The brave men, living and dead, who struggled here have consecrated it, far above our poor power to add or detract. The world will little note, nor long remember, what we say here, but it can never forget what they did here. It is for us the living, rather, to be dedicated here to the unfinished work which they who fought here have thus far so nobly advanced. It is rather for us to be here dedicated to the great task remaining before us, that from these honored dead we take increased devotion to that cause for which they gave the last full measure of devotion, that we here highly resolve that these dead shall not have died in vain, that this nation, under God, shall have a new birth of freedom, and that government of the people, by the people, for the people, shall not perish from the earth.
– Gettysburg Address, November 19, 1863

The Voter's Pledge

I will vote for candidates who are honest,
I will vote for candidates who tell the truth,
I will vote for candidates who will serve as models for my children,
for my grandchildren, and for future generations.

Endnotes

1   James P. Rowles, *Law and Agrarian Reform in Costa Rica* (Boulder, Colorado: Westview Press, 1985).

2   James Rowles, *El conflicto Honduras–El Salvador de 1969 y el orden jurídico internacional* (*The Honduras-El Salvador Conflict of 1969 and the International Legal Order*) (*San Jose: Editorial Universitaria Centroamericana* [EDUCA], 1980).

3   Karl Jaspers, *The Question of German Guilt*, New York: Fordham University Press, 2000 (E.B. Ashton transl.), 1947), 93.

4   José Otega Y Gasset, The Revolt of the Masses, paperback ed. (New York, W.W. Norton, 1964). Original Spanish ed. published in 1930. original W.W. Norton English ed. 1932

5   Robert D. Putnam, *Bowling Alone: The Collapse and Revival of American Community.* (New York: Simon and Schuster Paperbacks, rev. ed., 2000).

6   Tom Nichols, The Death of Expertise: *The Campaign Against Established Knowledge and Why It Matters*, 2nd ed. (New York: Oxford University Press, 2024).

7   Richard Hofstadter, *Anti-Intellectualism in American Life* (New York: 1966). *See also* Susan Jacoby, *The Age of American Unreason in a Culture of Lies*, 2nd ed. (New York: Vintage Books, 2018); and Matthew Motta, *Anti-Scientific Americans: The Prevalence, Origins, and Political Consequences of Anti-Intellectualism in the US* (New York: Oxford University Press, 2024).

8   Richard Haass, *The World: A Brief Introduction* (New York: Penguin Books, 2020), xv-xxii.

9   Franklin Foer, *World Without Mind: The Existential Threat of Big Tech* (New York: Penguin Press, 2017).

10 Timothy Snyder, *On Tyranny: Twenty Lessons from the Twentieth Century* (New York: Tim Duggan Books, an imprint of Crown Publishing, a subsidiary of Penguin Random House 2017), 65-71.

11 Snyder, On Tyranny, 65.

12 Snyder, 66-69.

13 See Victor Klemperer, *The Language of the Third Reich: LTI—Lingua Tertii Imperii— A Philologist's Notebook*, Martin Brody transl., Bloomsbury Revelations ed. (London: Bloomsbury, 2013).

14 Neil Postman, *Amusing Ourselves to Death: Public Discourse in the Age of Show Business*, 20th ed., New York: Penguin Books, 2006. This edition with a Foreword by Andrew Postman. [Originally published by Viking in 1985, and by Penguin Books in 1986.]

15 Postman, *Amusing Ourselves to Death*, 155-156.

16 *See* Melissa Murray and Andrew Weissmann, *The Trump Indictments: The Historic Charging Documents with Commentary* (New York: W.W. Norton & Company, 2024).

17 https://web.archive.org/web/20211016175441/https:/trenchantobserver.com/2021/02/16/memoriam-republican-party-march-20-1854-februart-13-2021/

18 https://web.archive.org/web/20210616234442/https:/trenchantobserver.com/2021/05/20/fascism-in-america-is-here-now-in-the-republican-party/

19 https://www.washingtonpost.com/opinions/2021/05/20/trump-republicans-violent-threats-election-2024/

20 https://web.archive.org/web/20210616222555/https:/trenchantobserver.com/2021/05/28/the-u-s-doesnt-need-investigations-or-commissions-it-needs-prosecutions/

21 https://www.bostonglobe.com/2021/01/04/opinion/trumps-crime-spree-must-not-escape-investigation/

22 https://www.washingtonpost.com/opinions/2021/08/05/heres-roadmap-justice-department-follow-investigating-trump

23 https://www.politico.com/news/magazine/2021/07/06/department-of-justice-january-6-capitol-riots-investigations-498253

24 https://web.archive.org/web/20210118210337/https:/trenchantobserver.com/2021/01/18/trumps-future/

25 https://www.washingtonpost.com/opinions/2021/08/05/heres-roadmap-justice-department-follow-investigating-trump/

26 https://www.bostonglobe.com/2021/08/20/opinion/merrick-garland-must-investigate-donald-trumps-attempted-coup-not-retribution-deterrence/

27 https://web.archive.org/web/20210616232550/https:/trenchantobserver.com/2021/06/06/29251/

28 https://www.cfr.org/blog/2020-election-numbers

29 https://www.nytimes.com/2021/01/07/us/politics/republicans-against-certification.html

30 https://www.vox.com/2021/1/6/22218058/republicans-objections-election-results

31 https://www.washingtonpost.com/opinions/2021/09/23/robert-kagan-constitutional-crisis/

32 https://www.tcm.com/tcmdb/title/27532/ship-of-fools#overview

33 https://www.wsj.com/articles/u-s-and-allies-look-at-potential-china-role-in-ending-ukraine-war-2d6cbb4d?mod=world_lead_pos2

34 https://trenchantobserver.com/2023/05/05/sudan-an-inspiring-story-of-two-student-taxicab-heroes-amidst-the-fighting/

35 https://trenchantobserver.com/2023/05/11/ukraine-war-may-12-2023-u-s-policy-on-territorial-concessions-in-ukraine-peremptory-norms-of-international-law-and-the-history-of-u-s-policy-for-the-last-90-years/

36 Edward Wong and Michael Crowley, "Ukraine's Offensive Could Set Stage for Diplomacy With Russia, U.S. Officials Say; While exploring endgames, Biden aides say they reject any push for peace talks — including from China — that would freeze the current front lines and Russia's gains," New York Times, May 12, 2023 (Updated 1:52 p.m. ET).

37 *See, e.g.,* James Rowles, "International Law and the structural impediments to a ceasefire or peace settlement in Ukraine," Trenchant Observations, November 8, 2022.

38 U.N. Charter, Art. 2 (4) provides:

> The Organization and its Members, in pursuit of the Purposes stated in Article 1, shall act in accordance with the following Principles.
>
> …
>
> (4) All Members shall refrain in their international relations from the threat or use of force against the territorial integrity or political independence of any state, or in any other manner inconsistent with the Purposes of the United Nations.

39 Vienna Convention on the Law of Treaties, Art. 52 codifies for all states the principle of non-recognition first contained in Article 11 of the 1933 Montevideo Convention on the Rights and Duties of States, which was applicable to the United States and countries in Latin America.

40 U.N. Convention on the Law of Treaties (1969), Art. 53, U.S. Stimson Doctrine, U.N. General Assembly Resolution 2625 (XXV), "Declaration on Principles of International Law Concerning Friendly Relations and Cooperation Among States in Accordance with the Charter of the United Nations (1970)" (hereafter "Declaration on Friendly Relations").

41 Art. 11 of the Montevideo Convention on the Rights and Duties of States 1933) establishes: The contracting states definitely establish as the rule of their conduct the precise obligation not to recognize territorial acquisitions or special advantages which have been obtained by force whether this consists in the employment of arms, in threatening diplomatic representations, or in any other effective coercive measure. The territory of a state is inviolable and may not be the object of military occupation nor of other measures of force imposed by a state directly or indirectly or for any motive whatever even temporarily.

42   Despite their illegality, U.S. interventions resumed during the Cold War, e.g.., in Guatemala (1954), Cuba (1961), the Dominican Republic (1965), Nicaragua (1981-1985), Grenada (1982)), and Panama (1989). The U.S. also intervened in Haiti in the 1990's. These interventions were generally of short duration except in Haiti and in the case of the covert war against Nicaragua. None involved any claim to the acquisition of territory.

43   The 1948 OAS Charter provides:

> Article 21
> The territory of a State is inviolable. It may not be the object , even temporarily, of military occupation or other measures of force taken by another State, directly ir indirectly, on any grounds whatever. No territorial acquisitions or special advantages obtained either by force or other means of coercion shall be recognized.

44   https://trenchantobserver.com/2023/05/11/ukraine-war-may-11-2023-britain-sends-long-range-missiles-to-ukraine-u-s-says-south-africa-sends-arms-to-russia-extraordinary-video-of-russian-soldier-pleading-for-mercy-and-being-escorted-by/

45   https://www.nytimes.com/2023/08/05/opinion/trump-coup-indict-trial.html

46   https://trenchantobserver.com/2021/06/02/sleepwalking-in-the-garden-of-fascism/

47   https://trenchantobserver.com/2021/09/23/our-democratic-house-is-on-fire/

48   https://www.nytimes.com/2023/08/06/world/europe/putins-forever-war.html

49   *See, e.g.,*

> 1) James Rowles,"We must defend Western Civilization as we follow its path into the future--Part One," Trenchant Observations, April 24, 2023.
> 2) James Rowles, "We must defend Western Civilization as we follow its path into the future--Part Two; The-fallacious thinking behind the 'New Multi-Polar International Order'," Trenchant Observations, April 25, 2023.
> 3) James Rowles, "We must defend Western Civilization as we follow its path into the future--Part Three," Trenchant Observations, April 25, 2023.

50   In this regard, see David Knowles, "Serhii Plokhy interview: 'Putin wants control of Ukraine – but he is prepared to go for plan B'; The celebrated historian and professor of Ukrainian history has studied the parallels between the 1930s and the years leading up to 2022," The Telegraph, July 9, 2023 (5:10 pm).

51   Roger Cohen, "Putin's Forever War," New York Times, August 6 2023

52   *See., e.g.,* Ishaan Tharoor, "Ukraine's hopes for maximal victory look remote," The Washington Post, August 21, 2023 (12:00 a.m. EDT).

53   https://trenchantobserver.com/2023/08/21/reprise-from-january-26-2022-reflections-on-czechoslovakia-1968-and-ukraine-2022-august-20-1968-dubcek-svoboda/

54   https://trenchantobserver.com/2023/08/17/ukraine-war-august-17-2023-le-monde-editorial-highlights-strategic-failures-of-the-west/

55   David French, "The Articulate Ignorance of Vivek Ramaswamy," New York Times, August 31, 2023, (3:00 p.m. ET),

56   See, e.g., Peter Segal, "The end will come for the cult of MAGA; The next generation isn't buying it," The Atlantic, August 30, 2023 (7:05 am ET).

57   https://trenchantobserver.com/2023/08/26/ukraine-war-august-26-2023-republican-unity-and-the-fascist-threat-of-trump-and-his-supporters/

58   Franklin Foer, "THE FINAL DAYS: Joe Biden was determined to get out of Afghanistan—no matter the cost, The Atlantic, August 29, 2023 (6 am ET).

59   Marc A. Thiessen, "Biden's disastrous pullout from Afghanistan could cost him reelection," Washington Post, August 28, 2023 (7:00 am EDT).

60   https://trenchantobserver.com/2023/09/11/ukraine-war-september-11-2023-bidens-failed-foreign-policy-leadership-the-west-and-the-global-south/

61   https://trenchantobserver.com/2023/09/09/ukraine-war-september-9-2023-bankruptcy-of-bidens-foreign-policy-revealed-in-g-20-communique-in-new-delhi/

62   *See, e.g.,*

    1) Carl Hulse, Luke Broadwater and Annie Karni, "McCarthy, Facing an Ouster and a Shutdown, Orders an Impeachment Inquiry; The move against President Biden, which Speaker Kevin McCarthy had been signaling for weeks, comes as some far-right House Republicans are irate over spending and threatening to depose him," New York Times, September 12, 2023 (Updated 6:55 pm ET).
    2) David French, "Where Is the Evidence, Speaker McCarthy?" New York Times, September 12, 2023.

63   Michael D. Shear, "Biden's Dog Bites Another Secret Service Officer; It is the latest in a series of episodes in which one of the family's pets has bitten people since the president took office," New York Times, September 26, 2023.

64   Marisa Inti, "Bidens' dog bites Secret Service officer in 11th known aggressive incident," Washington Post, September 27, 2023… (10:17 am EDT).

65   Shane Goldmacher, "Trump Leads in 5 Critical States as Voters Blast Biden, Times/Siena Poll Finds; Voters in battleground states said they trusted Donald J. Trump over President Biden on the economy, foreign policy and immigration, as Mr. Biden's multiracial base shows signs of fraying," New York Times, November 5, 2023.

66   A notable exception is David Axelrod, Barack Obama's campaign adviser, who while granting that the decision is Biden's to make has issued a thinly veiled call for Biden to withdraw from the race. *See,*

>   1) Hanna Panteck (Fox News), "David Axelrod doubles down on Biden criticism after president reportedly called him a 'prick'," New York Post, November 19, 2023 (2:03 p.m. ET);
>   2) Maureen Dowd, "The Axe Is Sharp," New York Times, November 18, 2023,

67   Ronald Brownstein, "How Biden Might Recover; The former president just revealed his plan to win a second term," The Atlantic, November 24, 2023 (6:00 am ET);

68   https://www.nytimes.com/2023/11/22/opinion/trump-danger-rage-psychology.html

69   Brian Klaas, "The Case for Amplifying Trump's Insanity; The 'Banality of Crazy' has warped American politics, as few voters recognize just how deranged, delusional, and dangerous Donald Trump is...because the press rarely reports on his routine insanity," The Garden of Forking Paths, October 1, 2023.

70   https://www.vox.com/2016/7/25/12270880/donald-trump-racist-racism-history

71   https://www.telegraph.co.uk/women/politics/donald-trump-sexism-tracker-worst-offensive-comments-quotes/

72   https://www.washingtonpost.com/politics/2023/07/19/trump-carroll-judge-rape/

73   https://www.npr.org/2023/09/29/1202534656/trump-fraud-ruling-new-york-business-empire-judge

74   https://www.theatlantic.com/national/archive/2023/08/washington-week-trump-indictments-gop-debate/674968/

75   https://www.washingtonpost.com/elections/2023/04/21/trump-agenda-policies-2024/

76   https://jamesrowles.substack.com/p/revised-and-updated-the-decline-of

77   https://jamesrowles.substack.com/p/2024-presidential-election-when-reason

78   https://www.theatlantic.com/ideas/archive/2023/12/ukraine-russia-war-aid/676287/

79   https://trenchantobserver.com/2023/09/27/as-the-global-south-turns-away-from-the-west-the-west-should-curtail-its-financial-support-and-trade-preferences-for-the-global-south/

80 https://trenchantobserver.com/2023/09/27/
ukraine-war-september-27-2023-experts-agree-the-international-order-is-crumbling/

81 David French, "The Case for Disqualifying Trump Is Strong," New York Times, January 4, 2024.

82 https://constitution.congress.gov/browse/amendment-14/section-3/

83 https://www.nytimes.com/2024/01/05/opinion/trump-supreme-court-colorado-ballot.html

84 https://substack.com/profile/29166244-michael-mauldin

85 https://substack.com/profile/96079507-james-rowles

86 *See, e.g.,* David A. Graham, "The Cases Against Trump: A Guide; Fraud. Hush money. Election subversion. Mar-a-Lago documents. One place to keep track of the presidential candidate's legal troubles," The Atlantic, January 17, 2024.

87 *See, also* Derek Hawkins and Nick Mourtoupalas, "Breaking down the 91 charges Trump faces in his four indictments," Washington Post, Updated August 15, 2023 (1:03 pm EDT).

88 *See, e.g.,* "Democracy on Trial," Frontline (PBS), January 30, 2024.

89 *See* James Rowles, "Trump appears barred by Section 3 of the 14th Amendment from running for president," Trenchant Observations, January 4, 2024.

90 *See* Alvin Chang, "The long list of Republicans who voted to reject election; List includes Ted Cruz of Texas and Josh Hawley of Missouri and a majority of Republican House member," The Telegraph, January 7, 2021;

91 *See, e.g.,* Anna Kaufmanm "The 2024 Senate elections are fast approaching. These are the seats up for re-election," USA Today updated September 8, 2023 (1:23 pm ET);

92 https://constitution.congress.gov/browse/amendment-14/section-3/

93 *See*

1) George T. Conway III, "The Court's Colorado Decision Wasn't About the Law; This case wasn't decided on its merits, and the result is an utterly flimsy legal argument, The Atlantic, March 5, 2024 (1:16 pm ET).
2) J. Michael Luttig and Laurence H. Tribe, "Supreme Betrayal: A requiem, The AtlanticMarch14, 2024.

94 See, e.g,, Thomas B.Edsall, "This Could Well Be Game Over'New York Times,March 6, 2024.

95 *See* note 80, above.

96 J. Michael Luttig and Laurence H. Tribe, "Supreme Betrayal: A requiem, The Atlantic, March 14, 2024.

97   Jack Nicas, "Brazil Bars Bolsonaro From Office for Election-Fraud Claims; Brazil's electoral court banned former President Jair Bolsonaro from seeking office until 2030 for spreading false claims about the nation's voting system," New York Times, June 30, 2023.

98   https://www.washingtonpost.com/opinions/2024/10/07/trump-immunity-judge-oct-7-anniversary-china-navy/

99   *See,*

> 1) Javier G. Cuesta y Antonia Sanchez-Vallejo, "Putin afirma que prefiere a Biden frente a Trump: "Es predecible"; El favorito de los republicanos para pelear por la Casa Blanca califica las palabras del líder ruso como "un gran cumplido", a la vez que defiende posturas que benefician a Moscú," El País, el 15 de febrero 2024 (21:19 CET):
> 2) Javier G. Cuesta and Antonia Sanchez-Vallejo, "Putin claims that he prefers Biden over Trump: "It's predictable"; The Republicans' favorite to fight for the White House describes the words of the Russian leader as 'a great compliment,' while defending positions which benefit Moscow," El País, February 15, 2024 (21:19 CET).

100   *See,*

> 1)Ann-Dorit Boy,"Der Meistertroll aus dem Kreml; Vermutlich meint Putin es ernst, wenn er sagt, ein US-Präsident Biden sei ihm lieber als einer namens Trump. Für den ist die Äußerung ein Geschenk," Der Spiegel, den 15. Februar 2024 (13.48 Uhr).
> 2) Ann-Dorit Boy, "The master troll from the Kremlin; Putin is probably serious when he says that he prefers a US President Biden to one named Trump. For him, the statement is a gift,", Der Spiegel, February 15, 2024 (1:48 p.m.).

101   https://jamesrowles.substack.com/p/in-a-country-with-no-memory-donald

102   https://jamesrowles.substack.com/p/disqualification-of-senators-josh

103   https://jamesrowles.substack.com/p/reprise-a-moment-for-reflection-the

104   James Rowles, "NUEVO—Europa cambió. El mundo cambió. El largo camino de guerra que tenemos por delante.; Recordando a Stefan Zweig, "El Mundo de Ayer" (1942)," Trenchant Observations, March 13, 2024.

105   *See* Patrick Wintour, "German living standards plummeted after Russia invaded Ukraine, say economists; Energy price shocks had huge knock-on effect, with real wages falling further in 2022 than in any year since 1950, says report," The Guardian, March 18, 202 (13:32 GMT).

106   See James Rowles, "With Ukraine on its back foot, it's time to take the war to Putin; Macron may be a flawed messenger, but he's got the right message," Trenchant Observations, March 8, 2024.

107 Nicolas Tenser, *Notre Guerre: L crime et l'oubli—pour une pensée stratégique* (Paris: Éditions de l'Observatoire/Humensis, 2024).

> *See also,*
> 1)Laure Mandeville, "Weit über die Ukraine hinaus ist etwas sehr viel Tiefgreifenderes im Gange": Der politische Philosoph Nicolas Tenzer erklärt den größten Fehler im strategischen Denken des Westens: die Annahme, dass Putin in der Ukraine einen klassischen territorialen Krieg führt. Und stellt klar, dass es eine Chance gegeben hätte, den russischen Machthaber von seinem Vorhaben abzuhalten," Die Welt, den 11. Februar 2024 (14:50 Uhr (Interview mit Nicholas Tenzer, Übersetzung von von Le Figaro);
> 2) Laure Mandeville, "'Far beyond Ukraine, something much more profound is going on"; The West must recognize the extent of the "total war" that Russia's ruler Vladimir Putin is leading against Ukraine, demands the French author and political philosopher Nicolas Tenzer in his book 'Notre guerre"," Die Welt, February 11, 2024 (2:50 p.m.). Interview with Nicolas Tenzer, translated from French article published in Le Figaro;
> 3) Laure Mandeville, "Nicolas Tenzer: 'La question du mal est une porte d'entrée pour l'analyse stratégique'," Le Figaro, le 1 février 2024 (18:57);
> 4) Laure Mandeville, "Nicolas Tenzer: 'The question of evil is a gateway to strategic analysis'," Le Figaro, February 1, 2024 (18:57).

108 *See* Stefan Zweig, *ThecWorld of Yesterday; Memories of a European.(1942)* (*Die Welt von Gestern; Erinnerungen eines Europäers, 1942).* For an excellent summary and critical review, see "The World of Yesterday: a brief review of a 1942 book," herthhub.eu, November 26 2022.

109 See, e.g., Philip Bump, "Robert Gates Thinks Joe Biden Hasn't Stopped Being Wrong for 40 Years," The Atlantic, January 7, 2014.

110 https://en.wikipedia.org/wiki/Michigan_House_of_Representatives

111 https://en.wikipedia.org/wiki/Michigan_Senate

112 https://www.nytimes.com/2024/07/16/us/politics/schiff-biden-democrats.html

113 https://www.nytimes.com/interactive/2024/07/12/opinion/biden-trump-electoral-map-outlook.html

114 https://open.substack.com/pub/jamesrowles/p/gavin-newson-and-gretchen-whitmer?r=1l7bf7&utm_campaign=post&utm_medium=web

115 https://www.wsj.com/articles/biden-cant-spin-his-way-out-of-this-age-decline-presidential-election-9df813d8

116 Quoted by Carl Hulse, Michael S. Schmidt, Reid J. Epstein, Peter Baker and Luke Broadwatein in their article, "Biden Called 'More Receptive' to Hearing Pleas to Step Aside; The president has given no indication that he is changing his mind about staying in the race but is said to be more willing to listen to the case for bowing out," New York Times, July 17, 2024 (updated 11:19 pm ET).

117 Tom Nichols, "The Truth About Trump's Press Conference; His obvious emotional instability is frightening, not funny, The Atlantic, August 9, 2024 (4:15 pm ET).

118 See,

> 1)Maggie Haberman, Shane Goldmacher, and Jonathan Swan,"Trump Tries to Wrestle Back Attention at Mar-a-Lago News Conference; In an hourlong exchange with reporters, the former president criticized Vice President Kamala Harris for not doing the same, insulted her intelligence and boasted about the size of his rallies," New York Times, August 8, 2024 (updated August 10, 2024 (10:24 am ET).
> *Note: The New York Times article was updated the morning after Nichol's column was published in The Atlantic.*
> 2)Michael Scherer, Jack Dawsey, and Patrick Svitek, "Trump holds meandering news conference, where he agrees to debate Harris; The Republican nominee made the announcement during an appearance where he made false or baseless claims as he sought to regain his footing against his Democratic rival, Washington Post, August 8, 2024 (Updated at 4:19 p.m. EDT).

119 https://www.washingtonpost.com/opinions/2024/08/16/newsletter-harris-election/

120 https://web.archive.org/web/20210612114756/https:/trenchantobserver.com/2021/06/02/sleepwalking-in-the-garden-of-fascism/

121 https://web.archive.org/web/20211027234810/https:/trenchantobserver.com/2021/09/23/our-democratic-house-is-on-fire/

122 https://www.azquotes.com/author/9962-H_L_Mencken

123 https://open.substack.com/pub/jamesrowles/p/public-discourse-in-america?r=1l7bf7&utm_campaign=post&utm_medium=web

124 https://www.wsj.com/us-news/springfield-ohio-pet-eating-claims-haitian-migrants-04598d48

125 https://www.youtube.com/watch?v=JMwgitYUp_g

126 https://www.npr.org/2024/09/15/nx-s1-5113140/vance-false-claims-haitian-migrants-pets

127 https://cidh.oas.org/countryrep/Haiti79eng/toc.htm

128 https://www.oas.org/en/iachr/reports/pdfs/2023/Informe_Haiti_EN.pdf

129 A terrific movie has been made about Jean Dominique, *The Agronomist: The true story of Jean Dominique, a Haitian radio journalist and human rights activist* (French, with English subtitles, 2003). The movie tells the dramatic story of Jean Dominique's life while revealing much about political and other conditions in Haiti.

130 https://www.hollywoodreporter.com/tv/tv-news/john-oliver-how-donald-trump-haitians-eating-cats-springfield-1236009137/

131 https://www.hollywoodreporter.com/tv/tv-news/john-oliver-how-donald-trump-haitians-eating-cats-springfield-1236009137/

132 https://news.yahoo.com/news/john-oliver-shreds-jd-vance-193430847.html

133 https://www.washingtonpost.com/politics/2024/10/11/trump-turns-immigration-closing-appeal-edge-economy-fades/

134 https://jamesrowles.substack.com/p/the-secret-brilliance-of-trumps-republican

135 https://jamesrowles.substack.com/p/satire-haitian-dogs-are-eating-white

136 *See* George F. Will, "World War III is already under way. Not that Harris or Trump has noticed; A new axis is sowing global disorder. The U.S. presidential campaign is what reckless disregard looks like, Washington Post, October 16, 2024 (2:23 p.m. EDT).]

137 *See*, e.g., Anne Appelbaum,"Trump Is Speaking Like Hitler, Stalin, and Mussolini; The former president has brought dehumanizing language into American presidential politics," The Atlantic, October 18, 2024 (6:00 a.m. ET);]

Acknowledgements

So many people have contributed to the development of my values, my sensibility, and my writing and analytical abilities, all of which made this book possible, that to thank them all would turn this Acknowledgments section into an autobiography. I cannot thank them all by name, but I want to express a special note of gratitude to those named below.

First of all, I want to thank Molly Faraji, my companion, whose love and support have benefitted my writing and the writing of this book in more ways than I can count.

I owe a particular debt of gratitude Michael Grossman, my book designer, who not only produced a great cover and interior design, but also responded quickly and proactively to all my questions, comments, and suggestions. I cannot imagine a more talented and dedicated book designer.

I owe a special debt of gratitude to Zaida Arguedas, my former wife, who accompanied and encouraged me in many ways, particularly during the writing of two books and numerous law review articles.

I also want to thank Edward M. Kovachy, Jr., my coach, who over the years manifested an unfailing appreciation of the quality of my writing and unshakable faith that this book would one day be published.

Special gratitude is due to Dr. Robert Louis Dodd, Stanford neurosurgeon *sans pareil* (without equal), without whose timely interventions this book might never have been written.

Michael Mauldin offered constant feedback and encouragement at the time each of these chapters was written. His comments, at times critical, helped me strengthen aspects of the articles that were weak or not fully developed. His steady encouragement spurred me on.

I also want to thank Joy Beeson, whose positive attitude after losing everything in the Paradise Fire (also known as the Camp Fire) in California in 2018 has been an inspiration, and whose encouraging comments on my columns, many of which make up this book, provided reassurance that I was writing something that was meaningful for my readers.

Mark Miller, whose artistic name is Octavious Sage and who is also known as Marcus Miller, provided such engaging intellectual interaction that we often lost track of time for hours in spirited conversation. His example as an author and an artist inspired me to reach for the highest goals. His painting, which adorns the cover, has captured in one visual image the heart of what this book is all about.

I also want to thank Gerard Lum, a friend and talented professional photographer, for his patience in our photo shoot and the author's final phtograph selected for the book.

In addition, I am grateful to Steve Murata, the leader of my Career Actions Ministry support group, for his constant encouragement and support for my writing endeavors over the years.

Stanford Law School classmates Alan Alhadeff, Jerry Halligan, John Mitchell, Dick Morningstar, Mike Roster, and Fred Smith offered encouragement and support in many ways for what turned out to be a long-term but fruitful endeavor.

Special thanks are due to Bill Wilby, lifelong friend who has followed the zigs and zags of my career over the years, providing encouragement and support which helped make this book possible.

Cynthia Travis and Larry Litt, fellow members of the Harvard Club of San Francisco Writer's Group, offered valuable feedback on different drafts and encouragement as this book was being written.

Also, I want to thank Russell Gonzaga and Rosie Llamado, constant participants in my Tracy Writer's Group, who provided valuable feedback on various writing exercises and encouragement of my writing.

Finally, I wish to acknowledge the enormous debt of gratitude I owe to three former mentors, who unfortunately are no longer with us today. Gordon A. Craig – perhaps the leading American historian of Germany for many years, was a model of what a great historian can be. Taking his courses and under his direction of my Senior Honors Thesis in History at Stanford, I learned much about the tragic history of Germany in the twentieth century and the phenomenon of pure evil in the form of Adolf Hitler and the Nazis during the Third Reich.

Professor John Henry Merryman of Stanford Law School was an inspirational teacher and mentor, who imbued in me a deep appreciation of the Civil Law Tradition which emerged from Rome, as well as as a deep interest in international development. His creative approach reshaped the study of Comparative Law in the United States, an approach which I myself used when I taught Comparative Law in law school settings. I also had the opportunity to work with him as a member of the Stanford Studies in Law and Development Project (SLADE) which he led (along with Professor Lawrence M. Friedman. Above all, he was a kind and understanding teacher who elicited excellence from me and from his other students.

At Harvard Law School I had the good fortune to persuade Abram Chayes to supervise my dissertation for the degree of Doctor of Juridical Science in International Law (S.J.D.). Abe, who I considered to be the greatest international lawyer of his generation, was a magnificent mentor and fantastic human being who showed deep compassion and understanding when I faced some of the hard vicissitudes of life. His approach to international law and his example continue to shape my understanding of international law not simply as a set of norms in books but rather as a vital instrument which can be used by individuals, officials, and governments to avoid and halt wars, defend the human rights of discrete human beings, and solve the many international challenges which the world faces. Abe was the State Department Legal Adviser in October 1962 during the

Cuban Missile Crisis which using international law he helped to defuse. He also led the drafting of arms control agreements which helped safeguard international peace and security for a generation. I will be forever grateful for his friendship and example.

About The Author

James P. Rowles is an author and international affairs columnist, and former law professor and international lawyer. He holds the advanced doctoral degree of Doctor of Juridical Science) in International Law (S.J.D.) from Harvard University, where he has taught human rights courses as a Lecturer on Law. He was also a Visiting Scholar at Harvard's Center for International Affairs (CFIA) and the recipient of a Harvard MacArthur Fellowship in International Peace and Security. Working in the field of international development, he served as Associate Director of International Programs at the Center for Criminal Justice (CCJ) at Harvard Law School,where he played a leading role in the development and implementation of a program of cooperation with the Guatemalan Judiciary during a hopeful period of civilian rule.

He has also taught international and comparative law courses at other universities, including Brandeis, the University of Pittsburgh, and the University of Kansas.

In addition, Dr. Rowles has worked as an international lawyer at a leading national law firm in Boston and at major global corporations on matters in Latin America, Europe, the Middle East, and Asia.

As an international development practitioner, he has worked on judicial reform, human rights, and access to justice projects in Latin America, Africa, the Middle East, Afghanistan, and Russia.

Early in his career, he was a senior staff attorney at the Inter-American Commission on Human Rights (IACHR) of the Organization of American States (OAS), in Washington, D.C. Dr. Rowles also was a recipient of the Rómulo Gallegos Fellowship in International Human Rights awarded by the Commission.

He received an A.B. in History from Stanford University, where he graduated "With Great Distinction" (*summa cum laude*). At Stanford, he won the James Birdsall Weter prize for the best senior honors thesis in history, which dealt with Germans' reexamination of their past after World War II.

He also received a J.D. (Juris Doctor, or Doctor of Law) from Stanford Law School, where his major concentration was in the areas of international and foreign and comparative law.

After graduating from law school, Dr. Rowles was a Stanford Postgraduate Fellow in Law and Development, working in Costa Rica as a Visiting Professor at the University of Costa Rica Faculty of Law, where he focused on law and development issues. In Costa Rica, he also worked as a member of the Costa Rican team of Stanford's Studies in Law and Development (SLADE) project, a six-nation study of law and social change in Costa Rica, Colombia, Peru, Chile, Spain, and Italy.

Upon returning to Stanford, he continued work on the SLADE project, wrote a thesis based on his research in Costa Rica, and obtained a Master of the Science of Law (J.S.M.=Ll.M.) in Comparative Law and Development.

Dr. Rowles has published two books and numerous articles on international and comparative law subjects. Since 2009, he has been the author of *The Trenchant Observer: International Law, Politics, and Security*, a blog which chronicles international political developments, with particular attention to the international legal aspects of these developments. *See* Preface regarding the availability on the Wayback Machine of the *Internet Archive* of articles from the blog, which has been hacked, probably by a state actor. Since 2022, he has been the author of *Trenchant Observations*, a Substack newsletter (https://jamesrowles.substack.com/).

He lives near San Francisco.

www.ingramcontent.com/pod-product-compliance
Lightning Source LLC
Chambersburg PA
CBHW051519150726
47997CB00001B/308